SUCCESSFUL
FINANCE

BRIAN BROWN

crimson

This edition first published in Great Britain 2009 by
Crimson Publishing, a division of Crimson Business Ltd
Westminster House
Kew Road
Richmond
Surrey
TW9 2ND

A catalogue record for this book is available from the British Library.

ISBN 978 1 85458 486 1

Printed and bound by Legoprint, SpA, Trento

CONTENTS

	Introduction	1
01	What does successful finance mean?	5
02	Identifying your costs	13
03	How to calculate and apply break-even positions	47
04	Preparing accurate and meaningful budgets	57
05	Managing the cash flowing through your business	95
06	Capital expenditure and managing capital resources	119
07	Understanding final accounts	135
08	Keeping a check on trends	151
09	Managing external financial influences	193
10	Quickstart guide: summary of key points	203
11	Troubleshooting	211
	Appendices	214
	Appendix A: Profit and loss accounts for StoneGlass Limited	214
	Appendix B: Balance sheet for years 2007 to 2009 (plus budget for 2010)	216
	Index	217

INTRODUCTION

Few businesses of any size achieve their maximum, or even optimum, profitability. Large businesses lose money through bureaucracy, departmental empire building and top-down mistrust. Small business owners and managers often lack the knowledge and time to identify and manage the important financial issues.

That is what this book is all about – finding easy and efficient ways to manage the financial aspects of the business in which you are involved, as a business owner, small business manager or large business departmental manager. The tools and processes that we suggest are equally applicable to non-profit organisations and to public institutions. If you want to make the best use of, and get the best results from, the money that flows through your organisation, this is the book for you.

This book is about understanding and working with financial information that is, or should be, available in your business. Therefore, we assume that your business already has accounting processes for recording financial information.

As we proceed through the book, we will provide real-life examples to illustrate how other businesses have dealt with particular issues; there are times when such examples will be anonymous to protect the guilty! We will also use a case study of a fictional business called StoneGlass, which is a family business (a father and three siblings) that has operated for some years and has begun to lose market share and profitability. Our intention when using StoneGlass is to demonstrate how another SMME (Small, Medium and Micro Enterprises) has tackled the problems it faces. Let us introduce you to this business:

Q CASE STUDY

StoneGlass Limited was set up by Bill Stone more than 20 years ago and has enjoyed successful growth over that time. The company produces specialist and artistic glassware such as vases and other coloured glass containers and, in recent years, has found particularly that foreign manufacturers have become major competitors. Bill's children have all gained qualifications and experience that the business could use, though Bill Stone is reluctant to change from the rather informal systems and processes that have sustained him over the years. However, in the face of falling profits he agrees to allow them to implement some reviews of the business. They start by looking at the resources now available to the business and produce the following action list:

- *The business needs to replace outdated production machinery with computer-assisted machines that give greater control over quality and are more cost-effective to run and maintain. The cost of purchasing these machines would be £635,000.*

- *The business needs to update its products by employing new artists or buying in freelance designs. A good designer would cost the business around £80,000 per annum; freelance designs can be commissioned at a cost of £10,000–£15,000 each. The business needs to introduce at least six new designs in the next year.*

- *The business has a permanent bank overdraft, limited to £250,000, which it regularly uses to support day-to-day activities. A new bank manager has indicated that she considers an overdraft facility to be an occasional buffer against seasonal imbalances rather than a regular fall-back and has asked the business to reconsider its financing arrangements.*

Having initially reviewed the business's financial requirements, the Stone family realises that it needs to raise around £1m to bring the business up to date and make it competitive again. StoneGlass approached its bank manager who said that she would not consider any future lending, including a bank overdraft, without a fully detailed business plan. After carrying out some research, the family found that, once a business plan had been produced, they would probably have access to the following options:

- *A loan of £1m from the merchant bank division of the current bank, repayable over 10 years at an interest rate of 8% per annum calculated on the balance outstanding at the beginning of each year.*

- *A loan of £1m from a venture capitalist, repayable over 10 years at an interest rate of 6% per annum calculated annually on the amount of the loan. The venture capitalist would also provide professional guidance to the business.*

StoneGlass's accounts for the last three years were available (this information is shown in Appendix A and we will deal with it later in the book). However, they now had to find all the financial information required for the business plan.

In addition to the StoneGlass case studies we will also provide opportunities, which we call 'Action points', for you to experiment with, to try a specific process in your business or check your understanding by engaging in an activity such as carrying out a calculation. We will not waste your valuable time by asking you to do frivolous or meaningless tasks – the activities will always help you to improve the financial performance for your area of responsibility. Therefore, you will get the best results from your reading by taking the few minutes required to complete activities as you come to them.

And, of course, because we have to deal with so many different financial issues in our jobs, it is good to have a source of reference for present and future emergencies, a constant point of reference is provided by this book.

Enjoy!

CHAPTER 1

What does successful finance mean?

The easy answer to the question posed in the heading is that successful finance means managing every aspect of your money to the best advantage. This means having:

- Enough money to buy the resources, or capital equipment, you need to produce the required level of business income.
- Cash to finance your ongoing business operation, including marketing and administration, while you are waiting for customers to pay you.
- Effective accounting records.
- Effective management of money within the business.
- Financial competitive advantage in relation to other similar businesses.
- The ability to apply forward planning to the financial function of the business.

SUCCESSFUL FINANCING

Successful financing is making sure that you have enough money in the business to implement your current and planned activities, and that you manage that money efficiently.

Graphically, successful financing can be shown as follows:

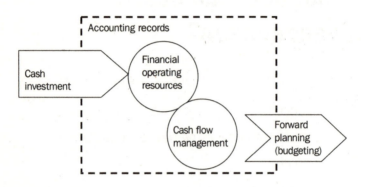

We will now go through each of these elements to understand what goes into having successful financing.

Cash investment

Cash investment is the fund that is made available to the business for the purchase of capital assets and planned future growth. Cash investment arises from:

- Money invested in the business by owners
- Money invested in the business by external investors
- Money obtained from loans or leasing arrangements
- Profits retained in the business

Financial operating resources

Managing the financial aspects of operating resources is usually referred to as 'managing the business' because it covers the operational activities of the organisation. The resources that have to be managed in most businesses include:

- Marketing and sale of products
- Purchase of materials, goods and services required by the business
- Maintenance of operational equipment
- Purchase and control of administrative activities, usually referred to as **overheads**
- Provision of cash, at the time required, to pay accounts. This is usually referred to as **cash flow**

ACTION POINT

This would be a good time for you to pause and list the processes that produce an income for your organisation (such as selling clothing or receiving an income from rents); and the activities for which you have to spend money (such as purchase of materials, payment of wages and cost of overheads). It is a good idea to list income items in a separate column from expense items.

Cash flow management

Cash flow management is the management of:
- Cash flowing into the business from sales of products
- Cash flowing out from the business to pay suppliers of goods and services.
- Shortfalls in cash requirements resulting from an imbalance between income and expenditure.
- Shortfalls in cash requirements as a result of failing to make a profit.

In accounting terms, this process is called management of **working capital** because it refers to the money, or capital, that is working in the business on a day-to-day basis.

TOP TIPS

Profitability and cash flow are different things, though they can be connected in some ways. Having a cash flow does not imply that the business is profitable, though making losses does reduce the flow of cash available. Making a profit does not imply having a cash flow if you cannot get your customers to pay their accounts.

Forward planning

Forward planning, in the form of **budgeting,** is absolutely essential for any organisation to be successful. In order to achieve a future objective you have to know what it will take to get there.

Q EXAMPLE

There is a point in the children's book Alice in Wonderland *when Alice arrives at a crossroads and meets one of the mad characters:*

'Excuse me, sir,' she asks, 'but could you tell me which way to go?'

'Where do you want to get to?' is the response.

'I do not know' says Alice.

'In which case it does not matter which way you go' replies the character.

The lesson here is that unless you identify where you want to get to, you probably will not arrive!

THE RELATIONSHIP BETWEEN INCOME, COSTS AND PROFIT

At its very basic level, investment capital is used to provide capital resources that produce the basic financial formula:

	Item:	Value (£):
	Income from Sales	1,000
Less:	Expenses	800
Equals:	Profit (distributed to investors or retained in the business)	200

TOP TIPS

In accounting jargon, income from sales can also be called 'revenue' or 'turnover'. Expenses are also called 'costs'.

In most organisations, the processes shown in this table are divided into three overall functions, which are:

- Producing an income or turnover to the business from sales and marketing activities. For a government department, this might be income from rates, taxes or levies.
- Creating the products ready for sale using the operating resources of the business.
- Managing the financial cash flow of the business.

Products that determine the income of a business can be:

- Goods that you manufacture for sale to other businesses or directly to the consumer
- Goods that you buy in for resale in your retail business
- Services that you provide to other businesses or consumers

In fact, a business can have good products and good operational functions but still might not be successful if the financial management does not operate effectively throughout the whole organisation.

🔍 EXAMPLE

Throughout the world, entrepreneurs see restaurant businesses as a good way to make money. They are relatively inexpensive to set up, have a high profit mark-up and enable the owner or chef to show his or her special skills. The problem is that chefs tend to be creative individuals who tend to overlook the importance of financial management. As a result, of all the new restaurants that open every year, 50% close within the first trading year and of the ones remaining, 50% will close in the second trading year. In January 2009, Gordon Ramsay, the famous TV chef, was fined for continually failing to submit and register the financial accounts for his restaurant chain.

(Source: Weekly Telegraph, 22–28 January 2009)

So, since business success is dependent on sound financial management, we need to find ways in which you can manage your business or department that will be effective and relatively easy to implement.

✊ ACTION POINT

Think about your business or area of responsibility. Is it a high-risk or low-risk type of business? In other words, what are the chances that your business could be replaced by another, better managed competitor business or operation? Access the internet and look for statistics that will tell you about the survival of your type of business. What do they tell you about the need for sound financial management?

QUICK RECAP

Successful finance means:
- *Identifying and acquiring funds for capital resources.*
- *Providing and managing the cash to finance ongoing operations.*
- *Keeping effective accounting records.*
- *Managing cash flow.*
- *Creating financial competitive advantage.*
- *Ensuring a balance between income, costs and profit.*
- *Planning for future operations and growth.*

CHAPTER 2

Identifying your costs

Every business must know its products and pricing structures. In order to get this information, you need to know the exact costs of running your business, which will include different trading processes, each of which involves costs related to:

- Producing your products or services for sale
- Delivering your products to the marketplace
- Marketing and selling your products
- Carrying out all the administrative activities required to control your business
- Paying for financial support

IDENTIFYING COSTS

 ACTION POINT

List every item on which you have to spend money for your business. Do not worry about writing down values at this time, but concentrate on listing every activity and every item you buy.

> **TOP TIPS**
>
> An organised way to identify all your costs is to go through each working day in your mind and visualise all the individual things that you do and every item that you use; list everything that costs money.

You can probably imagine that every business owner or manager will produce a different list of costs in reply to the above exercise but it is usual to categorise costs into certain groupings to enable different financial functions to be performed. But, before we explore the different categories, we need to explain the concept of **cost centres**.

COST CENTRES

A cost centre is the unit for which you are preparing a costing calculation. A cost centre can be a:

• Complete business.
• Department.
• Subsidiary business.
• Branch.
• Functional activity.
• Individual product.

This means that you can have a number of cost centres in your business. When you are calculating costs, you need to make sure that you identify exactly which cost centre you are focusing on. In the exercise above, you treated your business unit as a cost centre. The costs that you listed represented items according to when you use them but probably appear in a random order with some items perhaps appearing several times.

Traditionally, costs can be categorised in one of three different ways, which are:

- Capital costs and revenue costs.
- Direct costs and indirect costs.
- Fixed costs and variable costs.

Please note that we are not talking about specifying costs to specific categories – any cost can appear in each of the above categories. Costs can be divided into different categories according to your purpose. We show you how different categories of costs are used as we go through this chapter.

Capital Costs and Revenue Costs

The division between capital costs and revenue costs recognises the:

- Capital costs as the costs of purchasing the permanent or capital resources in the organisation.
- Revenue costs as the costs associated with running the business every day and generating value (sometimes known as running costs.

In financial management, we need to separate the costs of buying capital items that will last a long time, and the costs of running the business on a day-to-day basis. However, you need to be careful that you get your costs into the correct categories.

According to the above definition, you might list a photocopier as a capital cost since it will last a long time in the business. In fact you may need to consider how equipment is paid for in order to get a better picture of its true identity. For example, a photocopier that is leased or rented, rather than purchased outright is a revenue cost; a photocopier that is contracted on the basis of payment in accordance with the number of copies produced, is a revenue cost; a photocopier that is purchased outright using a loan from the bank is a capital cost.

If you own something that will be a permanent fixture in your organisation for a reasonably long time, even if you have borrowed money to pay for it, it is likely to be a capital cost. Having said that, there is one other 'convention' that you should be aware of when defining capital costs. By the definition given above, you could say that a pencil sharpener is bought outright and will be used by you for many years to come – therefore it must be a capital cost. While this is true in theory, it would not make sense to treat small items as capital expenditure because you would have an endless list of minor items that you would need to keep track of. The effort would not be worthwhile for such low cost items. You therefore need to think about such items in relation to the size of your organisation.

Q EXAMPLE

In a one-man courier business the purchase of electronic postal scales (about £250) probably would be a capital cost while the same scales purchased for use in the mailing department of a large retail organisation could be considered minor expense and therefore a revenue cost.

If you are in doubt about any cost in your organisation, you can contact HM Revenue and Customers for advice about the appropriate 'rule' for you.

Most SMMEs apply a cost limit or benchmark to capital expenditure; eg capital assets cost more than £1,000.

A business or department cost centre invariably contains a mixture of capital and revenue costs that can be shown graphically as follows:

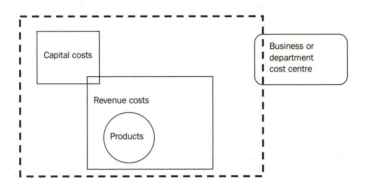

Revenue or running costs can now be divided into the other categories according to the purpose for which you want to use the costs in financial management.

Direct Costs and Indirect Costs

For most financial management processes, the costs of running your business unit on a day-to-day basis are analysed under the headings of direct and indirect costs:

- Direct costs are those costs that are absolutely necessary, or directly involved, in the production of your products.
- Indirect costs are the costs of supporting the product or service and are often associated with administrative processes.

Indirect costs are often called 'Overheads'.

🔍 EXAMPLE

In a restaurant, food to make up meals and the salary of the chefs preparing the meals are direct costs, while the salary of the bookkeeper who prepares the restaurant accounts is an overhead or indirect cost.

Some direct costs can be shared between a number of products, such as the timber in a furniture factory being used to produce both chairs and tables. Costs can also be partly 'direct' and partly 'indirect', such as a chef involved in preparing meals who is also partly responsible for supervising others, and some of his salary could be either a direct cost (preparing meals) or an indirect cost (supervising others).

Graphically, the division of direct and indirect costs can be shown as follows:

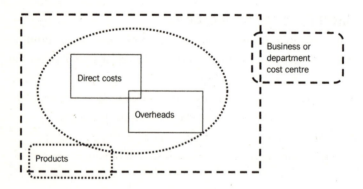

Notice how the division of direct and indirect costs is applied to different products as well as to different departments or to the business as a whole.

Indirect costs are usually difficult to apply directly to specific services; for example telephone calls can relate to different aspects of the business and insurance costs may similarly cover a whole range of risks. It is important that you categorise costs clearly and accurately, dividing or apportioning costs between categories so that you know the real costs of your business and your products.

ACTION POINT

This would be a good time to pause and revisit the list of costs that you wrote previously. Separate the listed costs into direct costs and indirect costs so that you are ready to add values to get your first financial statements together.

When a business is under financial or competitive pressure, it usually seeks to cut its indirect costs or overheads because it is usually much easier to reduce management and administrative costs than it is to reduce the direct operating costs that produce the business's products for sale. It is only when market demand is shrinking that it is able to reduce direct costs.

Costs in financial statements are often presented in the following format:

	£000s	£000s
Direct costs:		
Materials	1,378	
Workshop wages	893	
Packaging	127	
Power	210	
Delivery costs	89	
Total direct costs		2,697
Indirect costs (Overheads):		
Staff salaries	593	
Office light and heat	58	
Advertising	27	
Telephone and postages	8	
Stationery	3	
Insurances	14	
Bank charges	4	
Total overheads		707
Total costs		3,404

Notice how the columns have been headed to show that all the values in the tables are shown in thousands (£000s) and that group headings have been shown for the groups designated by lined boxes, such as the direct costs group (£2.697m) and the indirect costs group (£707,000) making a total costs value of £3.404m. This organisation will have to achieve sales or income in excess of £3.404m in order to show a profit.

TOP TIPS

Total direct costs are often represented in financial statements as 'Cost of sales' because they are the cost of creating products for sale by the business.

Revenue costs, including direct and indirect costs, can also be re-categorised into other groups called fixed costs and variable costs.

Fixed Costs and Variable Costs

Fixed costs are costs that remain constant, irrespective of changes in the level of production or sales (for example the rent on your business premises). **Variable costs** tend to vary, usually proportionally, to changes in the level of production or sales (such as the marketing budget).

TOP TIPS

Fixed costs are not necessarily fixed at a set rate forever, but usually remain at a set value for a long period of time such as one year.

Most businesses have fixed costs such as rent, business rates, leasing costs, insurance premiums, loan interest and staff salaries that are paid at a 'fixed' rate. These businesses also have variable costs that relate to how productive the business is and include materials used in production, production wages (including overtime), advertising, telephone charges, electricity, fuel, stationery and many other business expenses.

In a large organisation, fixed costs can be negotiated at a senior level and imposed on different departments or cost centres as part of a central management charge. In your department you may have to accept the imposition of this 'head office' fixed cost charge even though you may have little or no influence over what it contains!

Once negotiated, it is often difficult to change fixed costs even at very senior levels, so the business needs to be confident of the future when negotiating a commitment to fixed costs. Graphically, the analysis between fixed and variable costs for a cost centre can be shown as follows:

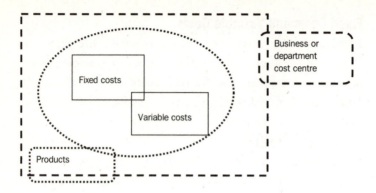

🔍 EXAMPLE

During 2007, a car retailer found that its business premises were not large enough and decided to move to larger premises. The owner negotiated a lease on a prestigious site because car sales had been buoyant for several years and the owner felt that he could easily afford a rental cost that was triple that of previous premises.

In 2008, credit crunch scares resulted in the withdrawal of easy car finance and the owner suddenly found that car sales fell by 30% and that he could no longer afford the larger premises. The landlord refused to cancel the lease agreement saying that the five-year lease agreement at the fixed rent should remain in place and the car retailer had a substantial fixed rent cost that had to be paid irrespective of how many cars he sold.

Costs are usually analysed between fixed and variable categories to enable us to calculate specific financial activities, such as a business's break-even point (which we deal with later).

ACTION POINT

Take the list of your costs when you analysed them into direct and indirect costs and, by the side of each item, indicate whether it is a fixed cost or a variable cost.

Q CASE STUDY

The Stone family knew that they must identify their exact business costs in preparation for the expansion they had in mind and started by creating a table to show how they categorised their costs.

	Capital	Revenue	Direct	Indirect	Fixed	Variable
Premises	■					
Machinery and equipment	■					
Office furniture	■					
Delivery vehicles	■					
Factory wages		■	■			■
Marketing and advertising		■	■			■
Staff salaries		■		■	■	
Directors' salaries		■		■	■	
Materials		■	■			■
Maintenance		■	■			■
Packaging		■	■			■
Council rates		■		■	■	
Electricity		■	■			■
Water		■		■		■
Telephone and postage		■		■		■

Stationery		■		■		■
Employee amenities		■		■		■
Insurance premiums		■	■		■	
Bank charges		■		■		■
Financial services		■		■	■	

Now that they had a list of the items to which they could add values the Stone family could now create an accurate list of expenditures.

Please note that the above list has been produced from the StoneGlass business's point of view. You may have similar costs that you have placed under different headings; your decision will probably be correct for your business unit.

Insurance premiums have been designated as a direct cost because StoneGlass's operational risks are associated with the production function. If the business insured very expensive computer equipment, the insurance premium might be applied as an indirect cost or it could be split between direct and indirect costs.

TOP TIPS

You have probably noticed that we have not tried to categorise capital costs into other categories. It is not usual to designate capital costs into other categories since we use categorisation in relation to operational processes and costs.

Your choice of categories will depend on what you are trying to understand from your work, and this will become clearer in the following chapters.

You could say that at the factory level, a StoneGlass quality supervisor's wages are a direct cost and variable because the work varies according to production levels. However, from a total business level the supervisor is probably paid at a fixed salary rate as a member of staff, so that this person becomes an indirect and fixed cost.

When you are trying to separate costs between the different categories to which they apply, you might need to use some form of cost apportionment.

APPORTIONING COSTS ACCURATELY

You can apportion costs in three different ways according to the factors:

• Space
• Machine capacities
• Employee working hours

Costs apportioned according to space used

When you apportion space costs, you compare the total number of square metres that an activity uses with the total number of square metres available. You start by calculating the total costs associated with the premises and dividing that total cost by the number of usable square metres in the premises, which gives you the cost per square metre. The formula for this calculation is:

$$\frac{\text{Total cost of premises}}{\text{Number of usable square metres}} = \text{Cost per square metre}$$

This 'cost per square metre' value can be used to measure and calculate the cost for any operational process.

🔍 EXAMPLE

Let us assume that you rent premises of 500 square metres for a total rental cost of £25,000 per annum, or £50 pa per square metre. If a certain process, such as a particular machine, occupies 100 square metres of the total space available, the rental cost of the machine's space could be apportioned as follows:

Rental cost of premises = £25,000 pa

$$\text{Rental cost of machine space} = \frac{£25,000 \times 100 \ m^2}{500m^2} = £5,000$$

You can use this process to calculate the proportion of the space used by each department as well as to allocate a cost for a particular machine or process, such as apportioning costs between production and administrative functions.

TOP TIPS

In the example used above, we apportioned only the rental costs of the space. You can carry out an apportionment calculation using the total cost of space available, including property rates, insurance, maintenance, and other premises costs.

Costs apportioned according to machine capacity

Capacity means the volume of production that a given machine can deliver and is calculated by dividing total machine costs by the number of items that the machine is capable of producing. This calculation is represented by the following formula:

$$\frac{\text{Total machine costs}}{\text{Number of products possible}} = \text{Capacity cost per item}$$

Total machine costs include the costs of buying, installing, maintaining, and running the machine and can also include a cost for the floor space used or taken up by a machine.

Q CASE STUDY

StoneGlass operates a moulding machine for 230 days each year for 8 hours each day; the machine is capable of producing 100 products per hour of operation. The costs of operating this machine are as follows:

Buying and maintaining the machine = £4,000 per annum or £2.20 per hour (£4,000 divided by 230 days x 8 hours)

10 square metres of floor space (calculated according to the information opposite) = £5,000 divided by 10 metres = £500 per annum or £0.28 per hour

Electricity to run the machine = £2,500 per annum or £1.36 per hour

Therefore, the apportioned cost of this machine per product produced, using the formula quoted above, is as shown in the following table:

	Per annum:	Per hour:
Purchase & Maintenance	4,000	2.17
Floor space	500	0.27
Electricity	2,500	1.36
Total costs	7,000	3.80
Capacity	184,000	100.00
Cost per product	0.04	0.04

Once you have calculated a 'capacity cost per item' for a machine, you can apply that cost to any product you produce using that machine.

Costs apportioned according to working hours

You calculate apportionment costs for the amount of time worked by an employee by dividing total employee costs by the total time worked. The formula for this calculation is as follows:

$$\frac{\text{Total employee costs}}{\text{Time worked in minutes}} = \text{Employee cost per minute}$$

Employee costs are usually calculated for a given period of time and include the following:

- Wage or salary.
- Statutory costs such as National Insurance payments.
- Pension contributions paid by the business.
- Other employee costs such as training costs.
- Cost of floor space used by the employee.

You can then allocate the resulting 'cost per minute' to a product according to the time taken to complete any task.

Q CASE STUDY

StoneGlass might calculate the employee cost per minute for polishing different products. For the 100 products produced by the machine in the example above, StoneGlass could have the following employee costs:

	Per annum:	Per hour:
Wage of machine operator	14,000	7.61
Wage of polisher	12,500	6.79
Statutory costs of above	1,855	1.01
Training costs	2,000	1.09
Floor space used	700	0.38
Total costs	31,055	16.88
Hours worked (2 employees)	3,680	2
Employee cost per hour	8.44	8.44

*You apply the concept of apportionment to accurately separate costs between direct and indirect categories. However, you have to apportion capital costs over their estimated lifetime; this process is called **depreciation**.*

CALCULATING DEPRECIATION

When you buy an expensive capital asset, you expect to use it in your business for several years and it would be inappropriate to apply the total cost of such an asset in just one trading year. A capital asset wears out gradually and its value diminishes as the years go on. Depreciation is the fall in value of an asset over time as a result of 'wear and tear'.

The time over which you depreciate an asset depends on the number of years that you expect it to operate in your business. For example, StoneGlass will probably expect to use its glass furnaces and glass forming machines longer that it would expect to use a desktop computer system.

HM Revenue and Customs has relatively straightforward guidelines that suggest:

- Most production machinery should be depreciated over a 10 year period.
- Computers and electronic equipment should be depreciated over three years.
- Vehicles should be depreciated over four years.

If you are uncertain about the time period over which you should depreciate a particular asset, you can get sound advice from HM Revenue and Customs (www.hmrc.gov.uk).

ACTION POINT

Go back to your list of capital assets and determine a depreciation period for each one. If you are in any doubt about a specific item, contact HM Revenue and Customs for guidance.

Traditionally, depreciation can be calculated in one of two ways, which are:

- Cumulative depreciation.
- Straight-line depreciation.

TOP TIPS

Whether depreciation is a direct cost or overhead will depend on the use of the asset being depreciated. If it applies to machinery used in producing products, it will be a direct cost; if the asset is used in the administrative process of the business, depreciation will be an overhead.

Cumulative depreciation

Cumulative depreciation recognises that, with care and good maintenance, an asset can last a lot longer than its assumed technical lifetime. For example, most businesses continue to use a computer system way beyond the 'accepted' three-year lifetime. Therefore, cumulative depreciation is calculated on the *remaining* value of an asset at the end of each year.

Q CASE STUDY

StoneGlass purchased production equipment in 2003 for £100,000 and determined a lifetime of 10 years. This means that the cumulative depreciation calculation for the equipment, up to the present, is as follows:

	Depreciation at 10% pa	Asset value (£)
Total cost at commissioning		100,000
2003	10,000	90,000
2004	9,000	81,000
2005	8,100	72,900
2006	7,290	65,610
2007	6,561	59,049
2008	5,905	53,144
2009	5,314	47,830
2010	4,783	43,047

The value of cumulative depreciation calculated for each year becomes less and less but the calculation continues beyond the 'normal' 10 year lifetime. However, the asset will never get to a point where it has no value because:

- It might be sold as a second-hand machine when the business no longer has a use for it.
- It can probably be sold for scrap once it is unusable.

A more popular way of apportioning depreciation, probably because it is far simpler to calculate and has a defined time period, is the system of straight-line depreciation

Straight-line depreciation

To demonstrate how straight-line depreciation works, we will again use the StoneGlass example of the machinery purchased in 2003 for £100,000, with an assumed lifetime period of 10 years. Using straight-line depreciation, the depreciation apportionment for each year will be one-tenth of the total costs of commissioning the machine, or bringing the machine into production.

Q EXAMPLE

The straight-line depreciation calculation for this machine is as follows:

	Depreciation at 10% pa	Asset value (£)
Total cost at commissioning		100,000
2003	10,000	90,000
2004	10,000	80,000
2005	10,000	70,000
2006	10,000	60,000
2007	10,000	50,000
2008	10,000	40,000
2009	10,000	30,000
2010	10,000	20,000
2011	10,000	10,000
2012	10,000	0

Therefore, at the end of the 10 year period, the asset has no accounting value in the records of the business. This does not mean that it cannot be sold in the future; it merely records that the business has 'written-off' the value of the purchase over 10 years. After that, any subsequent income received on the sale of the machine will be extra profit.

ACTION POINT

Compare the two types of depreciation apportionment and think about which calculation is the easiest to perform and which calculation provides a more realistic value at the end of each year for the type of assets that you employ in your business. Which system of depreciation is best for your business?

Because it is easier, most small businesses use the straight-line method for calculating depreciation. When you apportion costs as explained above, you are aiming to cost your products more accurately and therefore more competitively.

THE IMPORTANCE OF COMPETITIVE COSTING

If you speak with other business managers or owners, you might find that they ridicule the effort required to accurately apportion costs. For example, why bother to apportion the time the chef spends on cooking and supervision when you could just as well place the entire salary and other employee costs into overheads?

When you avoid apportioning costs accurately and enter them all into overheads, you are effectively dividing those costs between all products and applying them as a percentage addition in relation to direct costs. However, if you apportion your costs as accurately as possible, you know what each process in your business actually costs. Then many overheads can be allocated directly to a product rather than being transferred into a large overhead fund.

TOP TIPS

In some types of business it might be necessary to work in this way but in this case you need to be sure that costs are not misapplied into overheads and that the oversight does not make your business uncompetitive.

A larger or complex business might have a large number of indirect costs that would be difficult to apportion and apply to individual products. Accordingly, this type of business often lists indirect costs for one year and then calculates this total as a percentage of direct production costs for use when costing new products. However, this can make products uncompetitive since costs are not attached directly to relevant products so that each product fairly and directly carries all the costs related to that product.

Q EXAMPLE

A business that manufactures battery operated toys also makes battery chargers that it wants to sell as a separate 'add-on' product. The business treats the cost of producing sales invoices as an overhead which is applied as a percentage, between all products. This produces the following situation:

		Toy cost:	Charger cost:
	Direct costs of production	120.00	20.00
Plus:	Invoice overheads @ 10%	12.00	2.00
	Total costs	132.00	22.00

The business employs a part-time invoice clerk, at a cost of £1,000 per month, whose sole job is to prepare and send out 100 invoices each month. This means that the cost of sending each invoice is £10 (£1,000 divided by 100 invoices). Since we now know the cost of sending each invoice, we can apply that apportioned cost directly to each product as a direct cost rather than as a percentage overhead. The cost calculation now appears as follows:

		Toy cost:	Charger cost:
	Direct costs of production	120.00	20.00
Plus:	Invoice overheads @ £10	10.00	10.00
	Total costs	130.00	30.00

Each product now bears the true cost of invoicing. If the charger realistically costs more than a competitor, it could be more viable to buy this item in from specialist manufacturers.

However, you might have costs that cannot realistically be applied as direct costs but have to be included in overheads. You might need to calculate and apply the value of overheads as a proportion or percentage of direct costs.

CALCULATING OVERHEADS AS A PERCENTAGE OF DIRECT COSTS

We will return to StoneGlass to demonstrate how overheads can be applied as a percentage of direct costs.

Q CASE STUDY

StoneGlass's Profit and Loss Account for 2009 provides the following information:

	2009
Turnover	3,480,000
Direct costs:	
Materials	2,198,000
Wages	796,000
Employee costs	54,800
Maintenance	23,600
Electricity	18,100
Water	3,800
Consumables	8,300
Delivery costs	8,700
Business rates	18,600
Insurance	13,400
Total direct costs	3,153,300
Gross profit	326,700
Overheads:	
Owners salaries	180,000
Admin salaries	82,400
Employee costs	27,400
Design costs	
Marketing	8,100
Stationery	3,400
Telephone & post	7,600
Maintenance	1,700
Depreciation	10,000
Employee consumables	2,300
Loan interest	0
Audit	6,100

Bank charges	4,700
Total overheads	323,700
Net profit before tax	3,000
Less: Tax	4,000
Retained profit	−£1,000

The business has a number of different products that make it difficult to apply overheads directly, and it must find another way to deal with its direct costs of £3,153,300 and overheads of £323,700. To calculate the percentage variation between these two values, we apply the following formula:

$$\frac{Overheads}{Direct\ costs} \times 100 = Overheads\ as\ a\ percentage\ of\ direct\ costs$$

$$\frac{£323,700}{£3,153,300} \times 100 = 10.26\%$$

This means that when product costs are calculated, an uplift of 10.30% is applied to direct costs to cover the overheads.

This calculation is very straightforward, which is why some businesses choose this method. However, the calculation shown above is based on the costs for one year and applied to the following year, even though all costs change from year-to-year. The calculation assumes that the percentage increase calculated for one year will be similar for a future year, which is not always the case.

TOP TIPS

You rely on the accurate valuation of direct costs and overheads to calculate profit and selling price. Any error in your valuations can lead to incorrect selling prices and even perhaps selling products at a loss!

🖐 ACTION POINT

Think about your business and how you might have to apportion costs to accurately calculate direct costs and indirect costs. Make notes of the items you need to apportion and, if possible, calculate the apportionment you will use for your costings.

THE EFFECT OF UNCONTROLLED OVERHEADS

Some managers find it very tempting to start spending money on a 'wish-list' of things they have always wanted, such as the latest technology, fancy office furniture or a new high-performance car; some also aspire to having the largest department in the organisation, thinking that this makes them stand out as a successful manager. Of course, if you own the business there is no reason why you should not spend your money in any way you wish, but remember that when you increase your costs, and particularly your overheads, you are attacking your profits, or perhaps forcing up product prices to a possibly uncompetitive level.

Large organisations, and especially government departments, tend to employ more and more staff to deal with administrative processes. An increase in employees results in an increase in overhead costs because of extra salaries, additional statutory payments and the space needed by the new employees. Ultimately, senior management realise that the work of an overstaffed department can be done for a much lower cost by an external organisation, and employees working in that department are made redundant because the work is contracted out to the external organisation for a fraction of employee costs. This process is called **outsourcing.**

HOW TO USE DIFFERENT COSTING SYSTEMS

In order to calculate total costs accurately, especially when you are identifying the annual costs for a department or your entire business, you can use different systems, called **total absorption costing** and **marginal costing**.

Total Absorption Costing

Total absorption costing lists all costs to calculate the total cost (and thereafter a selling price) for a product or service or cost centre. By accurately identifying all costs, you ensure that you can meet all expenditures provided that you achieve the expected income levels. Total absorption costing means that you know that all your costs will be covered for a planned future period (usually one year).

TOP TIPS

Get into the habit of grouping costs into the direct costs and overheads categories. This will make it much easier when you have to prepare financial statements, budgets and cash flow statements later.

The StoneGlass information given previously is a good example:

	2009
Turnover	3,480,000
Direct costs:	
Materials	2,198,000
Wages	796,000
Employee costs	54,800
Maintenance	23,600
Electricity	18,100
Water	3,800
Consumables	8,300
Delivery costs	8,700
Business rates	18,600
Insurance	13,400
Total direct costs	3,153,300
Gross profit	326,700
Overheads:	
Owners salaries	180,000
Admin salaries	82,400
Employee costs	27,400
Design costs	
Marketing	8,100
Stationery	3,400
Telephone & post	7,600
Maintenance	1,700
Depreciation	10,000
Employee consumables	2,300
Loan interest	0
Audit	6,100
Bank charges	4,700
Total overheads	323,700
Net profit before tax	3,000
Less: Tax	4,000
Retained profit	–£1,000

Costs are grouped into direct and indirect categories and in total
provide a profit in relation to the total income achieved.

Q CASE STUDY

Bill Stone of StoneGlass is struck by an idea for a new product and implements absorption costing to determine what the new product would cost. He writes down a detailed list of the materials required and the time it would take to produce the product and lists the following costs:

Item:	Details:	£
Direct costs:		
Materials	Glass and chemicals	26.50
Wages		23.00
Employee costs		2.00
Maintenance and utilities		1.50
Consumables		0.50
Packaging costs		4.70
Rates and insurance		2.70
Total direct costs		60.90
Overheads:	10.26% on direct costs	6.25
Total costs		67.15
Profit mark-up	15% on total costs	10.07
Selling price	Ex factory	77.22

Bill Stone used the information from the business's accounting records to calculate direct costs, then added the mark-up for overheads previously calculated as a percentage of direct costs, plus an additional mark-up for profit, to arrive at a selling price.

ACTION POINT

Now you have a systematic way of listing your costs for a specific purpose, why not create a table similar to that shown above, and re-write your unit costs to work out a total cost for your department or business? How accurate do you think your income projection is? How healthy does your profit look?

Direct costs are sometimes referred to as 'cost of sales' in financial statements.

TOP TIPS

When you engage in total absorption costing, you calculate the costs related to the anticipated level of sales income. However, you might want to increase your level of business, from time to time, by offering special deals to customers. If you have accurately calculated your costs and selling prices, does that mean that you have to accept lower profits on those special offers? The answer depends on achieving your determined level of business.

Once you have achieved enough income to meet total costs, you may be able to accept lower prices for any additional work that you can attract and still achieve a similar or higher profit margin. How can this be?

This is because your fixed costs have already been covered in the planned workload.

Q CASE STUDY

Part way through 2009, StoneGlass knew that it had orders that would ensure it would reach its determined income of £3,480,000 and that its fixed costs would be met by the income achieved from the orders generated. Therefore, any additional business would not have to contribute to fixed costs, which had already have been paid for that year from known orders. It could cost additional orders using a process known as **marginal costing**.

Marginal Costing

TOP TIPS

Only engage in marginal costing once you are *certain* that the expected level of income and expenditure for your business will be achieved for the current year.

Marginal costing uses the fixed and variable costs categorisation because the calculation excludes fixed costs that have already been paid by existing business.

Q CASE STUDY

Using the table we produced earlier for StoneGlass, we can now produce the same information showing the fixed cost and variable cost categories.

	2009	Fixed costs	Variable costs
Direct costs:			
Materials	2,198,000		2,198,000
Wages	796,000		796,000
Employee costs	54,800		54,800
Maintenance	23,600		23,600
Depreciation		10,000	
Electricity	18,100		18,100
Water	3,800		3,800
Consumables	8,300		8,300
Delivery costs	8,700		8,700
Business rates	18,600	18,600	
Insurance	13,400	13,400	

Overheads:			
Owners salaries	180,000	180,000	
Admin salaries	82,400	82,400	
Employee costs	27,400	27,400	
Design costs			
Marketing	8,100		8,100
Stationery	3,400		3,400
Telephone & post	7,600		7,600
Maintenance	1,700		1,700
Employee consumables	2,300		2,300
Loan interest	0		0
Audit	6,100		6,100
Bank charges	4,700		4,700
Totals	3,477,000	331,800	3,145,200

Marginal costs are costs associated with additional work undertaken; another way of looking at this is that they are the costs that would be avoided if you did not undertake the additional business.

✎ ACTION POINT

If it would be useful for you to know the price levels at which you could take on extra work (in addition to the business level you originally projected), you now need to go back to your list(s) of costs and create a separate list for your business unit, dividing costs between fixed costs and variable costs.

Marginal costing starts by calculating the **contribution** made to the business as a result of taking on additional work:

Calculating business contribution

The formula for calculating contribution is as follows:

	Extra business:	£
	Income	XXX
Less:	Variable costs	X
Equals:	Contribution	XX

By producing extra products, total production and income is increased while total costs only increase by the variable costs associated with the extra work.

ACTION POINT

Take the list of fixed costs and variable costs and imagine that you increase your sales by 10% over your original projection. What price could you accept for that work and still achieve the same profit level? Re-calculate for a 15% extra output – what price do you have now? Does this give you an idea how some companies seem to be able to offer products at discount prices yet still produce good profits?

Q CASE STUDY

A major customer of StoneGlass offered to run a special promotion of the company's glassware by displaying £100,000 worth of products. However, to help it meet the costs of the promotion, the store requested a price discount of 15%. The Stone family knew that their normal profit mark-up was only 15% and thought they would have to refuse the extra business because it would give no profit. However, before doing so they decided to carry out a marginal costing of the order offered.

They first calculated the contribution that the order would make to the business:

	Extra business:	£
	Income	85,000
Less:	Variable costs	77,110
Equals:	Contribution	7,890

As a result of this calculation, the Stone family realised that they would make a profit of £7,890, or 9.3% on an additional order that they did not expect to have. They decided to accept the order in order to support a valued customer.

If you have products that sell extremely well yet you are not making the level of profit you expect, one reason might be that the high-selling (low priced?) products are actually under-priced because of poor costing.

In your working environment, any opportunity that you give to competitors to challenge the application of overheads could well mean that they can sell their products at a more competitive price!

ACTION POINT

Is this a good time to look again at your list of overhead costs? If you apportion as many of your overhead costs as possible directly against products or services, how does that make their cost look compared with your prior knowledge? Do you have any loss leaders you did not know about?

QUICK RECAP

- *Costs can be categorised into the following different groups:*
  - *Capital costs*
  - *Revenue costs*
  - *Direct costs*
  - *Indirect costs or overheads*
  - *Fixed costs*
  - *Variable costs*
- *Cost categories are not self-exclusive, but different categories are used for different purposes in financial management.*
- *Costing techniques help you to identify the relationship between income, the cost of producing a product, and the profit contributed to the business.*
- *Total Absorption Costing determines the overall total cost of a business unit or product.*
- *Marginal costing determines the contribution that additional orders make to the organisation.*

CHAPTER 3

How to calculate and apply break-even positions

If you work in a very dynamic, changing business environment, you will probably need to have a good idea of the break-even level – that is the point during a year at which operational or departmental costs are covered and the business unit moves from a loss situation into profitability. Using the total absorption method of costing, the calculation can be complex since it is necessary to allow for the fixed costs element at changing levels of output, month by month. To a large extent, it becomes a matter of trial and error, trying various values until a figure is reached *around which* the movement from loss to profit might occur.

In this chapter, we will show you how to calculate the break-even point for your business.

CALCULATING A BREAK-EVEN POSITION

An effective method for calculating break-even is to use the concept of contribution that we introduced in the previous chapter because break-even occurs when:

Total contribution = Fixed costs

Provided that you know the fixed costs and variable costs for a particular product, department or business, this calculation represents a much easier way of arriving at a break-even point!

🔍 EXAMPLE

A small business sells and installs CCTV front-door entry-phone systems for private consumers, for which it charges a standard price of £1,000 per system. Variable costs are £500 per installation and the business has fixed costs of £75,000 per annum.

The business calculates the contribution as follows:

	Per order:	£
	Income	1,000
Less:	Variable costs	500
Equals:	Contribution	500

Therefore, since we know that break-even occurs when total contribution equals fixed costs, we can say that, for this business, break-even will occur when it has completed enough orders to pay its fixed costs of £75,000. The formula for this calculation is:

$$\frac{Fixed\ costs}{Contribution} = Break\text{-}even$$

So in this case:

$$\frac{£75,000}{£500} = 150\ systems$$

The business owner now knows that the business will reach break-even once 150 orders have been completed and income of £150,000 has been achieved. After that point, each order will add £500 to business profits.

The break-even calculation shown above is relatively straight-forward because the business has one product. However, what happens if you have a complex business unit that has an income arising from multiple products or a mixture of products and services?

CALCULATING BREAK-EVEN FOR A COMPLEX BUSINESS

A complex or multi-product businesses might not be able to isolate individual products in order to carry out a related break-even calculation. For example, StoneGlass makes and sells a number of different products at various prices. In this situation, it is necessary to calculate a break-even point as a percentage of sales or as a break-even date within a trading period.

Q CASE STUDY

From the information previously calculated, the Stone family had the following information for 2009 that they could use to determine contribution for the year:

	Total: 2009	£
	Income	3,480,000
Less:	Variable costs	3,145,200
Equals:	Contribution	334,800

The 'standard' calculation for break-even would provide the following information:

$$\frac{\text{Fixed costs}}{\text{Contribution}} = \frac{£331,800}{£334,800} = £0.99$$

This has no meaning in terms of a break-even position. However, if we use that information as a percentage of income, we arrive at the following break-even point:

Income x 0.99 = £3,480,000 x 0.99 = £3,445,200

This means that, because StoneGlass's profit margin is so low, it will not achieve break-even until turnover reaches £3,445,200.

Another way of looking at break-even is to consider at what point, during a year, break-even will occur. The formula for this is as follows:

$$\text{Break-even} = \frac{\text{Fixed costs x 365}}{\text{Contribution}} = \frac{£351,800 \text{ x } 365}{£334,800} = \text{day 362}$$

This means that StoneGlass will break-even in 2009 during day number 362 in the trading year. Therefore, if the trading year starts on 1 January, break-even will not occur until 28 December. Please note that the late break-even point results from the very low profit made by the business in 2009.

🖊 ACTION POINT

If it would be useful for you to know where your break-even point occurs, calculate your break-even using the method given above. How does this feel to you? Is the break-even you have calculated a surprise to you? Will it help you in deciding the future direction of your business?

In order to allow for a minimum profit when you implement a break-even calculation, you can add a contingency allowance to the calculation.

ADDING A PROFIT CONTINGENCY TO A BREAK-EVEN CALCULATION

When you calculate your break-even point, you might want to ensure that:

- You are protected against cost inaccuracies or omissions.
- You are protected against potential price rises in variable costs.
- You provide some allowance for profit.

In this situation, you can amend the break-even calculations by incorporating a contingency allowance into the calculation of contribution, as follows:

	Per unit:	£
	Income	1,000
Less:	Variable costs	500
Less:	Contingency allowance	100
Equals:	Contribution	400

The contingency-protected break-even calculation for the business example above would then become:

$$\frac{\text{Fixed costs}}{\text{Contribution}} = \frac{£75,000}{£400} = 188 \text{ systems}$$

The business now has built-in contingency allowance of £100 per system or £18,800 up to the contingency-protected break-even point.

The break-even calculations shown so far are reasonably straightforward because they assume that the various costs and income figures used are stable and fixed. However, you may work in an environment where values – sales prices or costs – can change quite quickly. For example, as this book is being written, fuel prices are rather unstable and subject to change every few weeks. If you use a lot of fuel for your business, for example as a delivery courier would, you have to be concerned that your costs are likely to change significantly in the near future.

Continually re-calculating new break-even points to take into account changing values can be time-consuming and irritating, but there is a way of addressing this problem.

CREATING A BREAK-EVEN CHART FOR CHANGING VALUES

When changing values mean that you have to make several 'what if' calculations in order to determine different break-even positions, you may find it more convenient to use a **break-even chart**. For the security business that we used as an example previously, the break-even chart would appear as follows:

The following chart displays values in the traditional format, which shows:

- Units of output (orders received) along the horizontal axis.
- Values of income up the vertical axis.

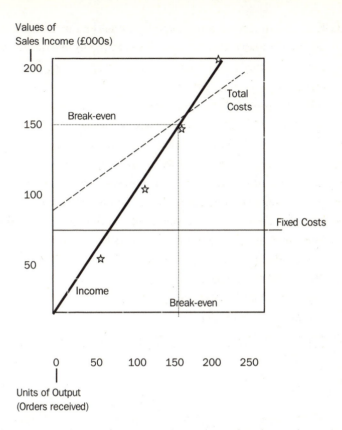

Values of
Sales Income (£000s)

Units of Output
(Orders received)

Since it can be confusing to take in how the above chart was completed, we will explain the processes, stage-by-stage, as follows:

1. Draw the line for fixed costs horizontally across the chart, running parallel to the base axis, and at a point on the sales income axis that represents the value of the fixed costs (£75,000).

2. Calculate the variable costs for each of the unit values along the bottom axis:

   50 units @ £500 each = £25,000
   100 units @ £500 each = £50,000
   150 units @ £500 each = £75,000
   200 units @ £500 each = £100,000

3. Calculate the total costs line (shown as the dotted line) by adding the above variable costs values to the fixed costs values for each of the 'units of output' and drawing the line for these values:

0 Units = 0 + £75,000 = £75,000
50 Units = £25,000 + £75,000 = £100,000
100 Units = £50,000 + £75,000 = £125,000
150 Units = £75,000 + £75,000 = £150,000
200 Units = £100,000 + £75,000 = £175,000

4. Finally draw the total income line (shown as the solid line with the stars) in a similar way starting at the zero point at the bottom of the chart and rising diagonally to join the income for each 'unit of output':

50 units @ £1,000 per unit = £50,000
100 units @ £1,000 per unit = £100,000
150 units @ £1,000 per unit = £150,000
200 units @ £1,000 per unit = £200,000

Having drawn all these lines, you can now identify the break-even point where the lines for total costs and income cross over each other. We have drawn finely dotted lines to show how break-even values can be read off on each axis - in this case break-even is £150,000 and/or 150 units. That is, break-even occurs when an income of £150,000 is achieved and/or when total output reaches 150 units (orders completed).

With this type of chart, you can draw as many lines as you wish (perhaps using different coloured pens) to illustrate changing values of cost or income, and then simply read off the values at the different break-even points.

Alternatively, if you have access to Microsoft Excel, or a similar programme, you can quickly create calculations that automatically update when you input different data.

QUICK RECAP

In this chapter, we showed you how to calculate:
- *Break-even points.*
- *A break-even point allowing for contingencies.*
- *Changing values for break-even using a break-even chart.*

CHAPTER 4

Preparing accurate and meaningful budgets

Depending on the size of your business, you may find maintaining control of expenditure both complex and difficult – how can you persuade everyone that actions they are used to performing, using materials they expect to have available, could perhaps be done more effectively using cheaper or fewer resources?

If you are to achieve a maximum profitability from your business, this level of control is very necessary, and you start by creating a sound budget. In this chapter, we will show you how to create budgets easily and improve the success of your business.

HOW DO BUDGETS ORIGINATE?

The head of every business unit must produce an accurate budget every year in preparation for each new trading year, to demonstrate how the unit will balance its income against its expenditure or costs and predict a contribution or profit.

Those responsible for meeting budgets should be the ones to create budgets.

TOP TIPS

A budget is an agreed financial fund sufficient to cover all the actions and resources for your business unit during an agreed period, usually one year. It states, 'If the business unit intends to produce a total output of £ xxx, we will require £ xx to cover the costs involved'.

A budget is usually drawn up using past experiences combined with a prediction or forecast of what should happen in the future; its aim is to ensure the best possible use of business resources to achieve given objectives. Individuals responsible for achieving a budget must positively contribute to the formulation of that budget, particularly when their performance will be measured against it.

ACTION POINT

Does your business create annual budgets at the moment? If so, who sets them? Do people in different sections of the business contribute to how budgets are made up? Do you think that your budgeting system is effective?

The areas covered by your budget depend on the function of the business unit for which you are responsible, but are likely to include:

- The volume of output of production or total revenues.
- Cost of materials needed to produce and service that level of output.
- Wages, salaries and statutory payments of employees.
- Cost of running the equipment resources that produce and support the work, such as lighting, power, stationery, telephones, etc.
- Cost of providing and maintaining the place of work, including rent, rates, insurance, cleaning, etc.
- Cost of support services such as personnel, medical, accounting, administration, security, etc.

A budget statement is usually formatted in a similar way to a P&L (profit & loss) Account and, for StoneGlass, is set out as follows:

	2009
Turnover	3,480,000
Direct costs:	
Materials	2,198,000
Wages	796,000
Employee costs	54,800
Maintenance	23,600
Electricity	18,100
Water	3,800
Consumables	8,300
Delivery costs	8,700
Business rates	18,600
Insurance	13,400
Total direct costs	3,153,300
Gross profit	326,700
Overheads:	
Owners salaries	180,000
Admin salaries	82,400
Employee costs	27,400
Design costs	
Marketing	8,100
Stationery	3,400
Telephone & post	7,600
Maintenance	1,700

Depreciation	10,000
Employee consumables	2,300
Loan interest	0
Audit	6,100
Bank charges	4,700
Total overheads	323,700
Net profit before tax	3,000
Less: Tax	4,000
Retained profit	–£1,000

TOP TIPS

This budget does not include any capital expenditure because capital expenditure is usually paid from retained profits or loans that are not part of the day-to-day operation of the business - the main focus in budgeting. Some businesses include an extra section at the bottom of the above table to show capital expenditure and source of finance for that expenditure. However, it is more common to have a separate Capital Expenditure Budget to cover that aspect of financial management.

You might assume that trying to predict the future means that budgets can only be 'guesstimates' of what might happen. Often, the formulation of a budget may have to take into account factors other than expenditure; for example an additional number of people required. In effect however, employing additional people translates into additional costs that you can include as monetary values in the budget calculation. If you are working in a large business, the budget for that business can be the total of the various departmental or business unit budgets produced by managers.

BUDGETING TECHNIQUES

Although some managers perceive budgeting as time-consuming and boring, it is a necessary part of the business's performance system and is directly related to profitability. If you allow your operating costs to increase over time, your business can spiral down into losses relatively quickly.

The categorisation of direct and indirect costs makes it easier to identify costs according to productive and administrative functions and budget statements are usually prepared using one of three techniques, called:

- Incremental budgeting
- Zero-based budgeting
- Flexed budgeting

Incremental Budgeting

Incremental budgeting involves taking the costs of the previous accounting period and adding percentage additions to cover:

- Increases in costs arising from higher purchasing costs or inflation.
- Increases in income and costs related to a predicted increase in business volume.

We can demonstrate what an incremental budget for StoneGlass would look like based on the 2009 data.

Q CASE STUDY

The Stone family decided to create an incremental budget based on the assumption that they would continue to use the current production facilities but would increase output and sales by 10%. They expected inflation to run at 5% for the coming year. Taking these factors into account they produce the following budget statement:

	2009	Business increase at 10%	Inflation increase at 5%	Budget 2010
Turnover	3,480,000	348,000	174,000	4,002,000
Direct costs:				
Materials	2,198,000	219,800	109,900	2,527,700

Wages	796,000	79,600	39,800	915,400
Employee costs	54,800	5,480	2,740	63,020
Maintenance	23,600	2,360	1,180	27,140
Depreciation	10,000	1,000	500	11,500
Electricity	18,100	1,810	905	20,815
Water	3,800	380	190	4,370
Consumables	8,300	830	415	9,545
Packaging costs	8,700	870	435	10,005
Business rates	18,600	1,860	930	21,390
Insurance	13,400	1,340	670	15,410
Total direct costs	3,153,300	315,330	157,665	3,626,295
Gross profit	326,700	32,670	16,335	375,705
Overheads:				
Owners salaries	180,000	18,000	9,000	207,000
Admin salaries	82,400	8,240	4,120	94,760
Employee costs	27,400	2,740	1,370	31,510
Design costs				
Marketing	8,100	810	405	9,315
Stationery	3,400	340	170	3,910
Telephone & post	7,600	760	380	8,740
Maintenance	1,700	170	85	1,955
Employee consumables	2,300	230	115	2,645
Loan interest	0	0	0	0
Audit	6,100	610	305	7,015
Bank charges	4,700	470	235	5,405
Total overheads	323,700	32,370	16,185	372,255
Net profit before tax	3,000	300	150	3,450

ACTION POINT

Is this the way you would expect to calculate a budget for your area of responsibility? What do you think the advantages and disadvantages of this technique might be?

In this example, the percentage uplifts for inflation and increased business have been applied to every item. You may already have realised that this can be questionable in some cases since an increase in business may not require a similar percentage increase in every cost item. For example, insurance and stationery would not necessarily cost any more just because business has been increased by 10%, and administration salaries would not be expected to cost proportionately more just because the volume of business has been increased.

This is the main problem with incremental budgeting systems - percentages get added 'across the board' which eventually results in higher overall costs, and subsequently sales prices that are no longer competitive in the marketplace. In some businesses, particularly in the public sector, next year's budget is calculated as a percentage uplift (to allow for inflation) on the amount spent this year. It has now become common for some public service bodies to 'squirrel away' excess money from their operating budgets to avoid losing the surplus. To pay for these excessive budgets, local rates then have to increase way beyond normal inflation rates.

🔍 EXAMPLE

Funds could be taken back from schools after ministers claimed last week that almost £2bn was lying unused in their bank accounts. The Government said action would be taken unless it saw a 'substantial reduction' in the amount of money hoarded by state schools. Some 20,462 out of 22,302 schools had surplus money – an average of £99,500 each. Chris Keates, the general secretary of the NASUWT union said, 'the point which is missed consistently by those who seek to defend the stockpiling of public money is that these funds are allocated each year to be spent on the pupils, not on either saving for a rainy day or to fund some state-of-the-art building project.'

(Source: Weekly Telegraph, 5-11 March 2009, "2bn unspent in school bank accounts", Graeme Paton, Education Editor

ACTION POINT

Is this the way your business works? What do you think the
outcomes might be of using this system?

When a budget is based on previous year's expenditure, there
is no incentive for any manager to save money from a business
unit's budget. The more spent in one year, the more money is
budgeted for the next. To achieve the best performance from your
business, it is important that every purchase is undertaken in the
most cost-effective way. You need to examine each purchase on
the basis of its value-for-money and value added to the business,
which involves:

• Negotiating the same level and quality of goods or services at
  a more advantageous price.
• Securing an increased level or quality of goods or services for
  the same cost.

This is probably what you would like to happen in your business
and you can achieve this level of efficiency using a system of value-
for-money analysis known as zero-based budgeting.

Zero-based Budgeting

As its name implies, zero-based budgeting starts from the
assumption that every cost has an assumed NIL or ZERO base,
and you question every item of expenditure in order to:

• Determine that the purchase is absolutely necessary.
• Investigate how it could be obtained in the most cost-
  effective way.

Clearly, checking every single cost on this basis can be a substantial
exercise initially, but it creates a budget database that is far easier
to manage afterwards. However, if this exercise appears to be too
overwhelming for you, you may choose to take a 'middle road'
approach to budgeting by:

• Taking your previous year's costs as a base.

- Investigating all costs that are:
  - Major contributors to your income-earning capacity.
  - High in relation to the overall budget.
  - In areas where you think you can make savings by negotiating better deals or changing suppliers.

You need to take into account known or anticipated increases in prices due to inflation, but you should assess these costs on an item-by-item basis rather than adding a 'standard' overall percentage increase to every cost. While suggesting a 'middle-of-the-road' option above, we still consider that it is vital to your business's success and to efficient financial management to apply the zero-based technique in your business as deeply as possible, asking the following questions:

- Can I justify this cost at all for next year?
- Could we do without this cost and still operate efficiently?
- If it is justified, how can I obtain each item at the most cost-effective price?
- Can I operate more efficiently without diminishing quality?
- Are there other good suppliers with lower prices and similar quality products and can I renegotiate the prices we pay?

Where large and increasing volumes of purchases are involved, you can often negotiate forward fixed-price contracts to create an accurate and more efficient budget. However, when you make the effort to calculate costs using a zero-based approach, this does not mean that you should dispense with 'common sense' - it is not cost-effective to spend a substantial amount of time investigating an item that costs a few pounds.

Never spend more, in terms of time and money, on investigating a cost than the potential saving achieved.

TOP TIPS

If a value is quite small you can treat it incrementally; if it is more substantial it could be worth your time and effort applying a zero-based technique.

Q CASE STUDY

The Stone family were uncomfortable with the incremental budget they had calculated and decided to try a zero-based approach. They produced the following alternative budget, still assuming that sales could be increased by 10% and inflation would run at 5%.

	2009	Business increase at 10%	Inflation increase at 5%	Budget 2010	Zero-Based adjustment	Budget 2010
Turnover	3,480,000	348,000	174,000	4,002,000	- 52,000	3,950,000
Direct costs:						
Materials	2,198,000	219,800	109,900	2,527,700	-17,700	2,510,000
Wages	796,000	79,600	39,800	915,400	- 65,400	850,000
Employee costs	54,800	5,480	2,740	63,020	- 6,020	57,000
Maintenance	23,600	2,360	1,180	27,140	0	27,140
Depreciation	10,000	1,000	500	11,500	0	11,500
Electricity	18,100	1,810	905	20,815	+ 500	21,315
Water	3,800	380	190	4,370	0	4,370
Consumables	8,300	830	415	9,545	- 445	9,100
Packaging costs	8,700	870	435	10,005	0	10,005
Business rates	18,600	1,860	930	21,390	+ 500	21,890
Insurance	13,400	1,340	670	15,410	- 410	15,000
Total direct costs	3,153,300	315,330	157,665	3,626,295	- 88,975	3,537,320
Gross profit	326,700	32,670	16,335	375,705	36,975	412,680

During the zero-based exercise, the Stone family found that certain budgeted costs, such as electricity and business rates, were not sufficient for the prices they were told would be applied in the coming year. However, other costs were over-estimated by applying the incremental approach. For example, since the business would not be employing more people to produce the additional products, the increase in wages and salaries would be a little more than the 5% allowed for the inflation increase; this made a substantial saving.

Overheads:						
Owners salaries	180,000	18,000	9,000	207,000	-18,000	189,000
Admin salaries	82,400	8,240	4,120	94,760	-4,760	90,000
Employee costs	27,400	2,740	1,370	31,510	-510	31,000
Design costs	0	0	0	0	0	0
Marketing	8,100	810	405	9,315	+500	9,815
Stationery	3,400	340	170	3,910	-310	3,600
Telephone & post	7,600	760	380	8,740	0	8,740
Maintenance	1,700	170	85	1,955	0	1,955
Employee consumables	2,300	230	115	2,645	-145	2,500
Loan interest	0	0	0	0	0	0
Audit	6,100	610	305	7,015	-315	6,700
Bank charges	4,700	470	235	5,405	-205	5,200
Total overheads	323,700	32,370	16,185	372,255	-23,745	348,510
Net profit before tax	3,000	300	150	3,450	60,720	64,170

Also, they were able to negotiate a saving in materials supplies because of the higher turnover and the supplier's fear that they would import foreign glass at a cheaper price. They also made small savings on items that would only increase by inflation irrespective of the increase in business volume.

As a result of the re-calculation of the budget on a zero-basis, StoneGlass was able to offer lower than expected sales prices to customers, giving them a competitive advantage, and still make more profit than they had anticipated under the incremental scheme.

Since zero-based costing assures you that every item of expenditure is necessary and is being obtained in the most cost-effective way, it also restrains you from building in a 'little extra' to cover 'just in case' situations.

ACTION POINT

Do you include some hidden allowances in your budgets, or is it common practice in your business? What are the advantages and disadvantages of having this hidden extra?

For many managers, this hidden allowance is an important part of the budgeting process, because events do occur that cannot be predicted. Such unexpected events can make it difficult to control ever-changing budgets, particularly if you work in a large business. What you need is some way of allowing for these 'unknown contingencies'.

Contingency Budgeting

To address the possibility of a future unknown event occurring, you can include an item called a **contingency allowance**, which is an additional cost to cover emergencies that might arise at some point in the future. However, the size of this allowance should be related to the:

- Overall size of the total budget.
- Type of function carried out by the business unit.

The work and costs of some functions do not change from day to day irrespective of quite dramatic changes in the business environment. Other functions that are directly influenced by dramatic changes may need extra resources to deal with them.

Q EXAMPLE

In the StoneGlass case study, the business has assumed an increase in turnover of 10%. In this situation, a stable function such as accounting is unlikely to require a contingency allowance because extra work will be minimal. However, it might be necessary to implement additional marketing to achieve the higher turnover in a down-turned economy. Therefore it could be desirable to include a contingency allowance to cover additional marketing, should it be required.

It is apparent that all budgeting functions, including contingency allowances, reflect knowledge from past experience coupled with a clear-sighted view of the future. However, you might question how you can possibly know about unknown emergencies that might arise in the future. In fact, most 'emergencies' tend to be the culmination of events that began much earlier, or even repeated from the past. With attention, it is possible to identify *now* the development of factors that you will call emergencies in the future, but you need a system for identifying factors that lead to 'emergencies' so that you can plan for them in the future. We call this tool a 'budget journal'.

ACTION POINT

Do you have any system for recording the day-to-day occurrences that you didn't expect or allow for? Have you experienced the realisation, 'that happened last year and I forgot all about it?'

Keeping a budget journal

The following example illustrates the origin and use of the budget journal.

🔍 EXAMPLE

A business operated in London, in the field of private medicine, has budgets calculated according to the number of patient appointments that could be filled during each working day.

Up to the current year, previous budgets had been poorly calculated and there was no record of past events, so it came as a surprise to a new manager when industrial action by London Underground personnel resulted in prospective patients not being able to get to the central London location. Underground trains did not run, buses were crowded and late, taxis were virtually unobtainable, and roads were jammed with people trying to keep appointments throughout the city. The result was that revenues for the duration of the strike were substantially reduced, to the point that they could not be retrieved during the remainder of the budgeted year.

During a discussion, long-term staff confirmed that they were aware that, in previous years, a London Underground strike often occurred at a similar time of year because wage negotiations usually began at a similar time of year and invariably broke down when the parties could not agree. The result was industrial action as a run-up to eventual agreement.

This event had not been remembered or mentioned when the budget was prepared. In order to prevent any future oversight of 'unexpected emergencies' the new manager introduced a budget journal to record events that had not been foreseen and built into the budget. When the next budget was created, the budget journal was the first record of reference to make sure that potential 'emergencies' were included.

When you use a budget journal, you can allow contingencies for future events that might impact on your business and the predicted accuracy of your budget is likely to be much higher, to the point when you are able to predict annual 'emergencies', often without using contingency allowances.

ACTION POINT

If you think that a budget journal could be a useful tool for you to adopt for your business, perhaps this is a good time to start one and record all the unexpected events of the past year that you can remember. Why not get other members of your staff to add their comments.

It is vital that everyone in the business understands and avoids the dangers presented by misused contingency allowances. It is human nature for a manager to try to 'play it safe' by inserting an over-large contingency allowance in a budget, but the practice can inflate costs and sales prices and make the business uncompetitive.

In some businesses, departmental budgets submitted to the head of finance are systematically cut without any valid reason other than, 'We know that managers allow contingencies so we cut them out by reducing all budgets submitted'. Managers get to know that whatever a budget says, the 'boss' or the finance department will always reduce it with little reference to the problems this might cause a manager who is trying to effectively manage his or her department on a reduced budget.

TOP TIPS

Budgets that are over-inflated by uncontrolled contingency costs, and budgets that are 'chopped' indiscriminately, both lead to the same result – a business that is not cost-effective and cannot be optimally competitive.

It is therefore extremely important that contingency allowances are well-founded and limited to very minor amounts in relation to the total budget. Make sure that everyone is made aware of how important accurate budget calculations are in relation to decision-making and future success.

TOP TIPS

If you allow budget contingencies, make sure that they are shown as separate items in the budget statement, with a note to explain why the contingency is required. Do not allow a manager to add a percentage to an existing cost. Highlighting the contingency for a specific purpose prevents it from being 'stolen' for another use.

Unfortunately, managers are tempted to prepare budgets that are 'safe rather than sorry' and to submit a relatively safe budget that can be achieved with ease. The business culture suggests that it is better to do that rather than to submit a challenging budget and then be blamed for failing to achieve it.

✎ ACTION POINT

Is this something you have done in the past or perhaps consider is reasonable for your business? What do you think are the advantages and disadvantages of 'safe' budgets? If you have subordinates who submit budgets to you, do you think that they submit 'safe' budgets? How does that make you feel? Are you the type of manager that cuts every budget submitted to you?

TOP TIPS

Ask yourself, 'Is it better to aim at 20% and achieve 25%, or to aim at 30% and achieve 28%?' In many businesses a manager in the first case would be praised and the second one reprimanded.

When a responsible manager looks at the coming year, he or she might well believe that the business unit could achieve better results, either in cost savings or higher output value, but might be reluctant to include higher values in case something unexpected happens to prevent the improvements. This happens particularly when:

- Achieving the improvement is dependent upon additional investment and the manager feels that the extra cost would be cut.
- Business performance is measured against specific budget outcomes as a benchmark for salary increases, bonuses or promotion opportunities.

In both cases, a manager can choose to 'play it safe', to the detriment of the business because 'safe' budgets do not present all the possible information to decision makers in the business, which means that they do not have the best information on which to make the best decisions. Adopting a 'safe budgeting' process removes the opportunity for you to make competitive decisions that could improve your profitability with the result that you achieve a lower level of success than you could have done using the fuller information. If managers budget for a minimum level of achievement, overall business growth is also minimised.

To overcome the mistrust that exists between managers and financial controllers, and to avoid excessive contingencies or budget cutting, we need another system of budgeting, called flexed budgeting.

Flexed Budgeting

You can get managers to provide 'real' information by demanding accurate information that everyone can trust and use. Flexed budgeting allows managers to accurately state budgets that give the following information:

- Achievable budget: based on a reasonable review of potential business and the likely movement in resource costs during the period, and in the current operating environment.

- Pessimistic budget: based on the impact that possible adverse external influences might have on the achievable budget.
- Optimistic budget: based on an objective view of the level of performance that *could* be achieved given the required level of support – people and resources – or the possible level of investment to harness potential growth areas.

As we will demonstrate below, this process does not actually involve three separate calculations, but works by 'flexing' the normal or achievable budget to create the others. Having access to information regarding the best and worst outcomes, decision makers can decide on the level of risk and expenditure they are willing to accept to achieve the most acceptable results.

Q EXAMPLE

A manager could use the optimistic budget to include additional sales that could be attracted by increased marketing expenditure. Senior management can then judge whether the higher cost justifies the extra business that might *be produced.*

The technique gives a manager the scope to put forward the most optimistic targets without the risk of 'blame' if they are not achieved. The manager would say, 'I am pretty sure I can make the achievable budget, but I have shown what the worst scenario might be and, with the identified support, I am willing to aim for the highest possible achievement!'

Q CASE STUDY

The Stone family looked at the zero-based budget and realised that it did not take into account what the business could achieve in a wider marketplace and with more investment in capital assets. They therefore decided to carry out a flexed budget exercise to identify their real options, and produced the following:

	2009	2010	2010	2010
	Actual	Minimum Budget	Standard Budget	Maximum Budget
Turnover	3,480,000	4,002,000	3,950,000	4,300,000
Direct costs:				
Materials	2,198,000	2,527,700	2,510,000	2,310,000
Wages	796,000	915,400	850,000	850,000
Employee costs	54,800	63,020	57,000	57,000
Maintenance	23,600	27,140	27,140	8,000
Depreciation	10,000	11,500	11,500	73,500
Electricity	18,100	20,815	21,315	18,000
Water	3,800	4,370	4,370	2,000
Consumables	8,300	9,545	9,100	4,000
Packaging costs	8,700	10,005	10,005	12,000
Business rates	18,600	21,390	21,890	22,000
Insurance	13,400	15,410	15,000	15,000
Total direct costs	3,153,300	3,626,295	3,537,320	3,371,500
Gross profit	326,700	375,705	412,680	928,500
Overheads:				
Owners salaries	180,000	207,000	189,000	200,000
Admin salaries	82,400	94,760	90,000	90,000
Employee costs	27,400	31,510	31,000	30,000
Design costs		0	0	80,000
Marketing	8,100	9,315	9,815	10,000
Stationery	3,400	3,910	3,600	3,000
Telephone & post	7,600	8,740	8,740	8,000
Maintenance	1,700	1,955	1,955	2,000
Employee consumables	2,300	2,645	2,500	1,000
Loan interest	0	0	0	80,000
Audit	6,100	7,015	6,700	7,000
Bank charges	4,700	5,405	5,200	5,000
Total overheads	323,700	372,255	348,510	516,000
Net profit before tax	3,000	3,450	64,170	412,500

Notes:
- *The increase in sales turnover has been identified as a result of talking with customers and identifying their needs. Some have already placed orders for the new designs.*
- *The increase in production arises from an investment of £635,000 for new machinery. This machinery works faster, uses less raw material and is environmentally friendly since it uses less electricity and less water. It will also require less maintenance.*
- *The budget not only relies on the capital investment but also on new designs. The Stone family have allowed £80,000 for the purchase of new designs from freelance designers.*
- *Capital investment will attract loan interest that has been included in the budget. Capital repayments will be made from profit.*

The Stone family can now decide how it will address the three options and whether it is willing to invest in substantial capital expenditure in order to achieve the maximum budget. It is not acceptable to 'chop' amounts from the budgets and expect the maximum return, because the three options show what is possible within the different ranges of criteria - if costs are cut, then the business will achieve only the lower level of success.

Financial management is only as good as the level of accuracy that you employ when you calculate financial values and the highest level of accuracy in budgeting recognises 'seasonal' variations.

Seasonally analysed budgeting

In order to prepare the way for the budgetary control process, which we deal with later, you must calculate budget figures that represent, as accurately as possible, the likely scenario that will develop in real time. You may need to account for any 'seasonalisation' likely to occur during the budget period. The most common seasonalisation is when income is directly related to the number of working days in each month. In this case, budgets should show changing values related to the number of working days, allowing also for public holidays and annual holiday closures.

Some engineering businesses have an annual holiday close-down period during which there is no production output (though there may be on-going costs). Garment manufacturers have 'seasons' when productivity is high, getting ready for the 'new season collection', followed by less productive times. In a multi-cultural society, it might be necessary to allow closures for important religious festivals for different religions.

Calculating budgets according to working days avoids the problem of having to investigate and explain why 'we haven't achieved this month's target because of the Easter Bank Holiday'.

If income is related to working days then there are likely to be costs that are similarly affected, such as power, materials and others. If your business is related to tourism, such as a hotel or restaurant in a holiday area, you should take into account the seasonal effect when some weeks or months, such as Christmas or July/August, produce substantially more business than other times.

🔍 CASE STUDY

Having accepted the maximum budget for 2010, StoneGlass decided to seasonalise the monthly values on the following basis:

- *Production and sales deliveries depended on the number of working days in each month.*
- *The company recognised the standard UK public holidays and closed between Christmas and New Year.*
- *The company closed its operations for three weeks during July, during which time machinery maintenance was carried out.*
- *Business rates and loan interest were paid in equal monthly amounts.*

- *Insurance premiums were paid on the first day of the year.*
- *Audit costs were paid on the last day of the year.*

StoneGlass calculated its number of working days for 2010 as follows:

	Jan	Feb	Mar	Apr	May	Jun	Jul	Aug	Sep	Oct	Nov	Dec
Days in month	31	28	31	30	31	30	31	31	30	31	30	31
Weekend days	10	8	8	8	10	8	9	9	8	10	8	8
Public holidays	1			2	2			1				2
Close-down							15					4
Working days	20	20	23	20	19	22	7	21	22	21	22	17

StoneGlass was able to produce the seasonally analysed budget for 2010 (based on a total of 234 working days for the year) to show:
- *Costs that move in proportion to income according to the number of working days in the month.*
- *Costs that are paid equally, usually monthly, during the year, such as salaries, business rates and loan interest.*
- *Costs that are paid at longer intervals, such as insurance paid annually.*
- *Costs that relate to specific events such as maintenance during the close-down period.*

This level of detail provides a good basis for the production of a cash flow forecast for the period, which we deal with later but, for the time being, you can quickly see that the StoneGlass seasonalised budget shows a profitable position for all months except July.

2010

	Year	Jan	Feb	Mar	Apr	May	Jun	Jul	Aug	Sep	Oct	Nov	Dec	Totals
Days:	234	20	20	23	20	19	22	7	21	22	21	22	17	234
Turnover	4,300,000	367,521	367,521	422,650	367,521	349,145	404,274	128,632	385,897	40,4274	385,897	404,274	312,393	4,300,000
Direct costs:														
Materials	2,310,000	197,436	197,436	227,051	197,436	187,564	217,179	69,103	207,308	217,179	207,308	217,179	167,821	2,310,000
Wages	850,000	72,650	72,650	83,547	72,650	69,017	79,915	25,427	76,282	79,915	76,282	79,915	61,752	850,000
Employee costs	57,000	4,872	4,872	5,603	4872	4,628	5,359	1705	5,115	5,359	5,115	5,359	4,141	57,000
Maintenance	8,000							8,000						8,000
Depreciation	73,500	6,282	6,282	7,224	6,282	5,968	6,910	2,199	6,596	6,910	6,596	6,910	5,340	73,500
Electricity	18,000	1,538	1,538	1,769	1538	1,462	1,692	538	1,615	1,692	1,615	1,692	1,308	18,000
Water	2,000	171	171	197	171	162	188	60	179	188	179	188	145	2,000
Consumables	4,000	342	342	393	342	325	376	120	359	376	359	376	291	4,000
Packaging costs	12,000	1,026	1,026	1,179	1,026	974	1,128	359	1,077	1,128	1,077	1,128	872	12,000
Business rates	22,000	1,833	1,833	1,833	1,833	1,833	1,833	1,833	1,833	1,833	1,833	1,833	1,833	22,000
Insurance	15,000	15,000												15,000
Total direct costs	3,371,500	301,150	286,150	328,797	286,150	271,934	314,581	109,344	300,365	314,581	300,365	314,581	243,502	3,371,500
Gross profit	928,500	66,372	81,372	93,853	81,372	77,212	89,692	19,288	85,532	89,692	85,532	89,692	68,891	928,500
Overheads:														
Owners salaries	200,000	16,667	16,667	16,667	16,667	16,667	16,667	16,667	16,667	16,667	16,667	16,667	16,667	200,000
Admin salaries	90,000	7,500	7,500	7,500	7,500	7,500	7,500	7,500	7,500	7,500	7,500	7,500	7,500	90,000
Employee costs	30,000	2,500	2,500	2,500	2,500	2,500	2,500	2,500	2,500	2,500	2,500	2,500	2,500	30,000
Design costs	80,000	6,838	6,838	7,863	6,838	6,496	7,521	2,393	7,179	7,521	7,179	7,521	5,812	80,000
Marketing	10,000	855	855	983	855	812	940	299	897	940	897	940	726	10,000
Stationery	3,000	256	256	295	256	244	282	90	269	282	269	282	218	3,000
Telephone & post	8,000	684	684	786	684	650	752	239	718	752	718	752	581	8,000
Maintenance	2,000	0	0					2,000						2,000
Emp consumables	1,000	85	85	98	85	81	94	30	90	94	90	94	73	1,000
Loan interest	80,000	6,667	6,667	6,667	6,667	6,667	6,667	6,667	6,667	6,667	6,667	6,667	6,667	80,000
Audit	7,000	0											7,000	7,000
Bank charges	5,000	427	427	491	427	406	470	150	449	470	449	470	363	5,000
Total overheads	516,000	42,479	42,479	43,850	42,479	42,021	43,393	38,534	42,936	43,393	42,936	43,393	48,107	516,000
Net profit before tax	412,500	23,893	38,893	50,002	38,893	35,190	46,299	-19,246	42,596	46,299	42,596	46,299	20,784	412,500

BUDGETARY CONTROL

There is absolutely no point in spending time and effort preparing a budget unless you intend to use it to control monthly operating costs. An accurate budget provides a sound basis for budgetary control, which is most effective when budgets have been 'seasonalised'. Budgetary control proceeds through the following stages:

1. Set standards and objectives by calculating an accurate budget.
2. Measure performance against budget by continually checking actual achieved figures against budget projections.
3. Identify areas for action by highlighting differences for investigation.
4. Take corrective action to bring the budget back into line.

These are not just one-off actions but form the budgetary control cycle, which is a continuous process that is repeated at the end of each month in most businesses. A diagram of the budgetary control cycle is provided below.

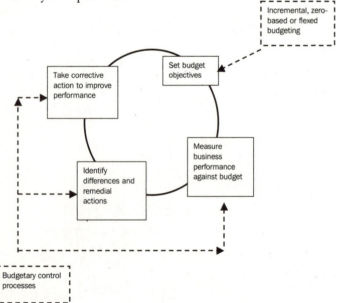

For budgetary control to be really effective, a number of conditions must exist within the business:

- The business's structure must be clearly defined, to identify responsibility for different budget centres.
- The budget manager's responsibility for creating a budget must be clearly defined.
- Managers must take an active part in originating and preparing budgets to ensure that they 'own the responsibility' for managing the budget.
- Business owners or senior managers must demand regular budget reports.
- The business must have a system for recording *actual* expenditure and income which is accurate, reliable and speedy.
- Actual expenditures must be published within a few days of the end of each month.
- The statement of actual income and costs must be produced to the budget format to enable managers to quickly identify, and act upon, budget variances.
- Budget monitoring must be carried out quickly to ensure that variances are quickly identified and dealt with.

TOP TIPS

A budget that is imposed on a manager will never be effective because (s)he will be able to say, 'I had nothing to do with this budget and it does not reflect the true circumstances of my business unit.'

ACTION POINT

Read through the above list and identify how many of the factors apply to your business. If there are any omissions, what effect do you think that might have on your business's ability to effectively manage budgets? What can you do to correct any anomalies?

Regular reporting of results is fundamental to any budgetary control system to enable corrective action to be quickly taken to bring the business back into line with budget targets. Review budgets monthly so that you can respond, at the earliest opportunity, to any adverse trend that appears. The following example shows how, in a dynamic market environment, the diligent checking of budgets produced the difference between success and failure!

🔍 EXAMPLE

In the early 1990s the airline industry came under severe business pressure due to:

- *An economic down-turn throughout Western countries.*
- *Conflict between the west and Gulf countries that increased the fear of terrorism and discouraged business travellers from flying internationally.*
- *Increasing competition and fare-cutting between airlines.*

As a result, profitability in the airline industry fell to the point where most major international airlines lost more money than they had made throughout their history. British Airways was adversely influenced by the decline in trans-Atlantic air traffic but had a strong commitment to budgetary control and quickly spotted the declining trend. The company quickly implemented actions to counter the decline by:

- *Withdrawing from 'loss-leader' price cutting.*
- *Taking action to reduce costs.*
- *Delaying investment in planned developments.*

As a result, British Airways was the only major airline to make profits during that period.

The monthly budgetary control statements produced by a business are often referred to as **management accounts**.

To enable you to take timely and positive action, you use a process called variance analysis.

HOW TO IMPLEMENT A VARIANCE ANALYSIS PROCESS

When differences or variances from budget occur, you should investigate every one, whether good and bad, to determine how each difference has occurred and how it might impact on profitability. An inspection of 'variances-from-budget' quickly identifies when things are not going as planned and gives you the opportunity to take remedial action before too much damage occurs. Managers can be tempted to look only at larger, or adverse variances because these cause greatest concern, but such 'cherry-picking' ignores the possibilities that:

- Repeated small variances can add up to large deficiencies over a period of time.
- Positive variances can indicate a change in the marketplace that needs your action to maximise the opportunity.
- Positive and negative variances might balance each other out but for safety's sake you need to understand what is happening.

It is important that you understand the reason(s) for all variances so that you are aware of everything influencing the performance of your business.

Q CASE STUDY

StoneGlass implemented budgetary control and produced monthly checks of actual performance against budget. The result, for February, showed the following information:

	Budget:	Actual:	Variance:	
	Feb	Feb	Feb	Comment:
Days:	20			
Turnover	367,521	348,230	19,291	Discounted sales to clear old stocks
Direct costs:				
Materials	197,436	203,780	-6,344	Make up of short deliveries in January
Wages	72,650	72,650	0	
Employee costs	4,872	4,872	0	
Maintenance		190	-190	New circuit breakers for extra machines
Depreciation	6,282	6,282	0	
Electricity	1,538	1,530	8	
Water	171	180	-9	
Consumables	342	340	2	
Packaging costs	1,026	1,010	16	Unexpected price increase – plastic tape
Business rates	1,833	1,833	0	
Insurance			0	
Total direct costs	286,150	292,667		
Gross profit	81,372	55,563		

Overheads:				
Owners salaries	16,667	16,667	0	
Admin salaries	7,500	7,500	0	
Employee costs	2,500	2,500	0	
Design costs	6,838	13,500	-6,662	2 designs delivered in 1 month
Marketing	855	1,700	-845	Delay in January marketing
Stationery	256	0	256	Over-ordered for discount in January
Telephone & post	684	700	-16	Employee under investigation
Maintenance	0	0	0	
Empl. consumables	85	80	5	
Loan interest	6,667	6,667	0	
Audit	0	0	0	
Bank charges	427	430	-3	
Total overheads	42,479	49,744		
Net profit before tax	38,893	5,819		

On investigation, the Stone family could explain most variances, but were concerned about two items:

- The unexpected price increase for packaging tape, though a new supplier was quickly identified who could supply at the expected price.
- The unexplained increase in telephone costs. An employee was concerned about the health of her mother, who lived in Spain, and had used the business telephone. The employee agreed to repay the cost of the calls.

Other than these items, the family were satisfied that other differences related to a 'roll-over' from the previous month.

The Stone family were satisfied that they understood how and why all the variances had occurred and had taken actions to protect the business. However, they had to check that:

- The fall in turnover was really a result of selling old stock at discounted prices and not the beginning of a trend in falling sales values.
- Deliveries of materials returned to the expected schedule to protect the smooth operation of the production function.
- The prices of packaging tape did not begin to escalate from the new supplier.
- Marketing processes were controlled to ensure that marketing input reinforced the predicted sales volumes.
- Over-ordering of stationery was not a 'scam' to get a 'free gift'.
- The use of the business telephone for private calls, without permission, had been stopped.

In other words, a responsible manager would investigate ALL variances, good and bad, to determine why they have occurred and whether they might influence, or be influenced by, future budget periods. The manager might have to adopt a 'Sherlock Holmes' attitude to seek out the clues, particularly from junior staff trying to cover up errors. Where very small variances occur, you have to decide at what level you will investigate because you also have to avoid falling into the trap of the investigation costing more than the variance.

ACTION POINT

Do you have a policy for identifying and addressing variations to monthly budgets? At what level do you expect yourself or managers to investigate variances? Are positive variances investigated? In the light of the information given above, would this be a good time to stop and write notes for a revised budget policy to ensure that your business identifies ALL the relevant information produced by budget analysis?

However, some variances will appear now but will disappear over time, such as the purchase of stationery at a good price now, to be stored for future use - an immediate 'over-spend' gradually disappears as the stationery is used up.

StoneGlass's budgets include a report explaining variance from budget and this report becomes very repetitive when explaining a self-correcting variance over several months. It is more beneficial, and presents a more accurate picture, if the budget control process shows actual results against budgets for the:

- Current month or budget period.
- Accumulated period from the beginning of the year up to and including the current month or budget period.

This can be achieved through a process called cumulative budget analysis.

Cumulative budget analysis

In the StoneGlass case study above, the variance analysis raised several questions, some of which suggested that the variance could be the result of expenditure over a longer period than the month of February. This arises because expenditure can be brought forward or delayed so that actual costs appear in a different period from that budgeted. The use of cumulative budget analysis can help you to identify the effects of actions that are 'out of sync' with original budget periods by showing:

- The variance analysis for the period under review.
- The variance analysis for the cumulative budgets for the operating year-to-date.

Another very important function of this system is that it helps to clarify factors that are showing an ongoing trend, so that it not only helps you to identify a variance for the latest month but also shows if that variance is repeated from earlier months; you can quickly observe any emerging pattern through the cumulative period.

Q CASE STUDY

Recognising that the budget prepared did not present all of the relevant information, it was decided to produce cumulative budget analyses for the business. The February analysis is shown in the following table:

	Budget: Yr-to-Jan	Actual: Yr-to-Jan	Variance: Yr-to-Jan	Budget: Feb	Actual: Feb	Variance: Feb	Budget: Yr-to-date	Actual: Yr-to-date	Variance: Yr-to-date	Comments:
Days:	20			20			40			
Turnover	367,521	371,320	-3,799	367,521	348,230	19,291	735,043	719,550	15,493	Jan - good. Feb – discounted sales
Direct costs:										
Materials	197,436	188,960	8,476	197,436	203,780	-6,344	394,872	392,740	2,132	Saving with new machines
Wages	72,650	72,650	0	72,650	72,650	0	145,299	145,300	-1	
Employee costs	4,872	4,872	0	4,872	4,872	0	9,744	9,744	0	
Maintenance	0	0	0	0	190	-190	0	190	-190	New contact breakers
Depreciation	6,282	6,282	0	6,282	6,282	0	12,564	12,564	0	
Electricity	1,538	1,541	-3	1,538	1,530	8	3,077	3,071	6	
Water	171	169	2	171	180	-9	342	349	-7	
Consumables	342	345	-3	342	340	2	684	685	-1	
Packaging costs	1,026	1,055	-29	1,026	1,010	16	2,051	2,065	-14	Jan supplier price corrected
Business rates	1,833	1,833	0	1,833	1,833	0	3,667	3,666	1	
Insurance	15,000	15,000	0	15,000	15,000	0	15,000	15,000	0	
Total direct costs	301,150	292,707		286,150	292,667		587,299	585,374		
Gross profit	66,372	78,613		81,372	55,563		147,744	134,176		
Overheads:										
Owners salaries	16,667	16,667	0	16,667	16,667	0	33,333	33,334	-1	
Admin salaries	7,500	7,500	0	7,500	7,500	0	15,000	15,000	0	
Employee costs	2,500	2,500	0	2,500	2,500	0	5,000	5,000	0	
Design costs	6,838	0	6,838	6,838	13,500	-6,662	13,675	13,500	175	Lower charge from designer
Marketing	855	0	855	855	1,700	-845	1,709	1,700	9	
Stationery	256	500	-244	256	0	256	513	500	13	Bulk purchase
Telephone & post	684	721	-37	684	700	-16	1,368	1,421	-53	Employee use – resolved
Maintenance	0	0	0	0	0	0	0	0	0	
Empl. Consumables	85	87	-2	85	80	5	171	167	4	
Loan interest	6,667	6,667	0	6,667	6,667	0	13,333	13,334	-1	
Audit	0	0	0	0	0	0	0	0	0	
Bank charges	427	420	7	427	430	-3	855	850	5	
Total overheads	42,479	35,062		42,479	49,744		84,957	84,806		
Net profit before tax	23,893	43,551		38,893	5,819		62,786	49,370		

As a result of using cumulative analysis, the Stone family were able to 'rationalise' issues that flowed from month to month and quickly identify ongoing variances that needed to be addressed. Issues causing concern from the single month's analysis were corrected in the cumulative analysis, resulting in less time being needed for investigation.

Of equal importance is the opportunity to identify continuing variances resulting from a change in market factors, which can have a dramatic effect on business results. The British Airways example showed that the earlier you identify such trends the faster you can make relevant decisions to protect business profits.

Q CASE STUDY

StoneGlass has sales periods when sales were higher than expected and when lower income was achieved because of the disposal of old stocks at discounted prices. The question is whether the higher sales figure achieved is a change in the marketplace that needs to be supported by higher production. In this case, the business has to consider its stocks and materials ordering policy and also check to see that employees and cash reserves can support the extra level of production.

ACTION POINT

Do you use cumulative analysis in your business? Do you receive monthly reports from managers explaining variances from budget? How closely do you check that the information you receive has been thoroughly investigated and nothing is being covered up? Do you get budget reports within seven days of the end of each month? Do you need to change your budgetary control system to protect your business from undiagnosed problems?

Budget monitoring is of little use unless it identifies variances quickly and you must make sure that:

- Actual income and expenditure accounting is updated weekly and summarised within three or four working days of the end of the month.
- Budget reports from managers are completed within seven working days of the month end.
- Remedial actions are identified and addressed within 10 working days of the month end.

We need to address one further question about budgets – do you amend a budget when you find that events are not in line with your predictions?

CHANGING BUDGET VALUES

TOP TIPS

Because a budget is a *prediction* of what you consider to be the most likely pattern of operation for a year, it can never be totally correct.

Since a budget is an accurate prediction rather than a statement of actual events, it is also a learning tool – you use a budget and budgetary control to learn the finer points about the internal operation of your business and the oddities of marketplace movements.

In many businesses, senior managers have an idealised view of how the various departments operate, sometimes issuing an operational manual to determine how processes should be carried out. When managers and operatives are not involved in creating budgets, senior managers use their idealised perceptions to create budgets 'as they see them'. In reality, the employees at working level often find better ways of working and 'short-circuit' laid-down operating procedures more efficiently. When this happens, budgetary control processes identify a number of 'unexpected' variances.

Should budgets be amended to take into account the variances that occur each month? The answer to that is a resounding 'No!' because changing the budget covers up errors built into the original budget and results in inefficient budgets being set in the future.

TOP TIPS

In business where budgets are used to measure personal performance, leading to the awarding of bonuses (especially in the public sector), budgets are often amended monthly to 'correct' the variances that appear. The aim is to end up with a 'correct' budget to show how well the business unit has performed and that it is worthy of the bonus.

Budgets should never be changed during a normal trading year in any business. The process of identifying and addressing variances should be used as a learning tool to encourage budget-makers to access the information available at every level in the business when setting the next budget.

However, there are very occasional events that impact on a budget to such an extent that they render a budget meaningless, including the following:

- Take-over of, or merger with, another business.
- Disruption of a major part of the business by fire or storm damage.
- Close-down of a business for health and safety reasons.
- Total and unexpected elimination of the business's marketplace.

For example:

- Businesses were destroyed by the New Orleans floods in 2007 and business customers were drastically reduced.

- Dunfermline Building Society was taken over by Nationwide in 2009.
- The Riverside restaurant was closed because of suspected food poisoning in 2008.
- The new car market collapsed in 2009, which meant that businesses supplying new cars had to offer huge discounts to make any sales at all.

The examples show that these businesses would have found it impossible to continue using budgets that had become meaningless as a result of the changes experienced. In any one of these circumstances, it would be necessary to set a new budget to reflect the changed circumstances.

TOP TIPS

Once agreed and set, budgets should only change when they have been overtaken by **substantial, unexpected and dramatic** events.

Budgets should *never* be changed because they have not been met in the normal course of business. Unless you can clearly identify where you have gone wrong, you will never get it right!

ACTION POINT

Do you have a policy for changing budgeted values? Do managers of business units change budget values at will in order to demonstrate a better performance than they have actually achieved? Would this be a good time to re-write and publish a new policy outlawing any budget changing at business unit level?

QUICK RECAP

- *A budget is a plan outlining the expected total costs of providing a specific level of products in the next trading period.*
- *Incremental budgeting involves adding percentage uplifts to a previous year's figures to take account of inflation and additional projected business.*
- *Zero-based budgeting assumes a nil base for future costs and examines whether expenditure is necessary and, if so, how it can be implemented most cost effectively.*
- *Contingency budgeting is a way of allowing for unexpected emergencies in the future.*
- *A budget journal is a tool for recording unexpected events so that potential repeats can be allowed for in subsequent budgets.*
- *The indiscriminate cutting of well-prepared budgets can create a barrier to business growth and profitability.*
- *Flexed budgeting provides maximum information to enable decision-makers to achieve optimal results.*
- *Seasonally analysed budgets provide accurate costs to reflect other seasonal variances.*
- *Budgetary control aims to check that a business unit has:*
  - *Achieved the projected level of income.*
  - *Not exceeded the projected level of expenditure.*
- *An effective budgetary control system includes a repetitive cycle of actions, including:*
  - *Setting budget objectives.*
  - *Measuring actual performance against budget standards.*
  - *Identifying areas for remedial action.*
  - *Taking necessary action to correct unexpected trends.*
- *To support an effective budgetary control system, you first need to implement a number of basic requirements, such as:*
  - *Involvement of departmental managers in the preparation of budgets.*
  - *An accurate, reliable and timely system for recording and disseminating actual financial information.*

- *Regular monitoring.*
- *Willingness to investigate variances.*

- *The budgetary control cycle is most effectively implemented by the use of variance analysis and particularly of cumulative budget analysis*

- *In the normal course of business, budget values should* never *be changed.*

CHAPTER 5

Managing the cash flowing through your business

You generate profits by implementing sound costing, budgets and budgetary control. You generate cash flow, or the money flowing into and out from your business, through efficient management of working capital. Poor cash flow management can result in your business failing so it is not enough to sell your products, you also have to make sure that you get paid for them. The following chapter shows the difference between generating profits and generating cash flow, and how to manage your cash flow successfully.

DIFFERENCE BETWEEN PROFITS AND CASH FLOW

The following example outlines the difference between generating profits and generating cash flow:

Q EXAMPLE

The following table shows the same situation in different circumstances:

Scenario 1:	Accounts: £	Cash: £	Credit: £
Total sales	100,000	100,000	0
Total costs	70,000	50,000	20,000
Positive cash flow	30,000	50,000	20,000

Scenario 2:	Accounts: £	Cash: £	Credit: £
Total sales	100,000	0	100,000
Total costs	70,000	50,000	20,000
Negative cash flow	30,000	50,000	80,000

Sales, costs and accounting cash flow are the same in both scenarios, but actual cash flow is very different – in Scenario 1, there is a positive cash flow, or an excess of income over expenditure, of £50,000 and in Scenario 2 there is a negative cash flow, or an excess of expenditure over income, of £50,000.

MANAGING WORKING CAPITAL

Working capital is the money used to finance your day-to-day activities, which is the cash that you have in your bank account and the money that is committed to the following:

• Stocks of production materials, part-finished products, products ready for sale and administrative materials such as stationery.

- Money owed by customers.
- Cash floats in a petty-cash box or shop till.
- Money owed to suppliers.
- Bank overdrafts and short-term loans.

TOP TIPS

Stocks of production materials and part-finished products, or work-in-progress, are often grouped together under the heading of 'inventory'.

🔍 CASE STUDY

StoneGlass' working capital is listed on its balance sheet for 2009 as follows:

Current assets:	£	£1,184,500
Stocks	492,000	
Debtors	692,500	
Cash in bank account	0	
Current liabilities:	£	£777,600
Creditors	528,600	
Bank overdraft	249,000	
Surplus of working capital		406,900

Positive accounting figures do not necessarily mean positive cash flow. StoneGlass is able to operate smoothly provided that debtors pay their accounts on time to enable the business to pay its creditors on time and the bank does not ask the business to repay its overdraft. If the above account showed a deficit of working capital, StoneGlass would not have the cash available to pay its creditors and might have to arrange a higher overdraft, a long-term loan or sell a capital asset to get cash into the business.

To ensure that you have control of working capital, you have to manage all the elements of it, starting with managing your inventory.

MANAGING INVENTORY

Some businesses, particularly in the retail sector, record the movement of stocks through shop tills or other computer programmes. Each time a product is sold, the till deducts it from the stock level and shows the number of items still remaining in stock.

TOP TIPS Most businesses today use a specialist stock management computer programme, or adapt the Excel programme, to manage inventory. However, not having access to a computer is not an excuse for failing to manage your inventory effectively.

If you do not have computer support for your stock control, you can record stock movements using a stock control record such as the following:

Stock No: A110 Item: 25 mm Glass pellets (25 kilo bags) Supplier: ABC Glass Supplies Ltd.			
Date:	Quantity in:	Quantity out:	Balance:
01.03.08	100		100
07.03.08		20	80

This system gives you a record for each item in stock and allows you to display information such as supplier details. This card is fixed to the storage location where the item is stored and is used to record movements in stock quantities to record the following:

• When goods are received, the date and quantity are entered on the correct card and the balance increased.

- When goods are taken from stores, the date and quantity are entered on the correct card and the balance remaining in stock reduced.

In theory, stock control record cards should always show the correct quantities of each item in stock. However, we can all make mistakes that might affect the accuracy of the numbers shown, by:

- Failing to record items received into stores.
- Failing to record items withdrawn from stores.
- Entering transactions onto the wrong cards.
- Entering transactions incorrectly.
- Losing or destroying cards so that there is no record of certain stock items.

Because mistakes are possible, you should continually monitor the accuracy of stock control records.

🔍 EXAMPLE

A new aero-supplies stores clerk was instructed to check six items every day, starting with fighter jets stored in a hangar ready to replace out of service aircraft. He found that the numbers stored were short of the number on the record card by one jet. The clerk systematically checked stock movements going back over three years and found that previous clerks had assumed that something as large as a fighter jet could never go missing – a proper stock check had not been carried out for at least three years! In fact, the source of the error was never discovered – the business had lost a fighter jet worth millions of US dollars!

You also have to carry out an annual stock check of all items in storage at the end of every trading year in order to provide an accurate value of stocks for end-of-year accounts.

In addition to effective control of stocks, you must make sure that you have sufficient stocks to meet operational needs, which means:

- Sufficient materials are available to feed production machines.
- Retail outlets have sufficient stocks to meet customer needs.

Maintaining stocks to meet operational requirements

Efficient financial management means always having enough stock available to keep your business working, which should take the following factors into account:

- Volume of materials you use daily.
- Minimum volume of materials you need to order from a supplier. For example, the glass pellets shown in the example record above are packed in 25 kilo bags and the supplier might demand a minimum order of 100 bags.
- Lead time required to process and deliver an order, which includes:
  - Time for orders to get to the supplier.
  - Supplier's processing and administration time.
  - Supplier's manufacturing or assembly time.
  - Delivery time from supplier to you.
- Possibility of supply shortages resulting from market forces.
- Shelf life.

The increase in building and construction projects over the last few years caused a shortage in the availability of steel, copper pipe and plaster board dry walling. In the food retailing sector, fresh food products deteriorate very quickly and food retailers try not to over-order supplies that go off and have to be thrown away.

ACTION POINT

What materials do you use in your business? What lead-times do they have from major suppliers? Are your suppliers influenced by demand pressures from much larger businesses or overseas buyers? Are there any materials on your list that deteriorate very quickly? How long would you have to use these materials before they became waste? How much do these factors impact on the stock levels you have to keep?

Clearly, you have to take into account all factors that might affect your ability to obtain sufficient quantities of materials to keep your business running smoothly. The following example demonstrates a system or formula for calculating optimum stock quantities.

🔍 CASE STUDY

StoneGlass uses glass pellets at the rate of 20 bags each day and ABC Glass Supplies Ltd require customers to order in minimum quantities of 100 bags; it also takes a minimum of two weeks to process and deliver an order. This means that StoneGlass must have stocks of glass pellets that will last at least two weeks and calculates its stocks levels as follows:

	Bags:
10 working days @ 20 bags	200
Allowance for late delivery = 5 working days @ 20 bags	100
Minimum stock quantity	300
Supplier lead time = 10 working days @ 20 bags	200
Maximum stock quantity	500

Minimum and maximum stock quantities are recorded on the stock record card so that the person responsible re-orders supplies when the quantity in stock falls below 300 bags.

Your aim is to have enough stock to keep the business operating smoothly, but not such high levels of stock that you have cash tied up unnecessarily.

🔍 EXAMPLE

Large businesses often use high quantities of materials and the stocks that they keep for normal business activities cost a great deal of money. In the 1970s, the car manufacturing industry negotiated a new system with suppliers in order to minimise the amount of money required to finance high stock levels. This system is called Just–in–time (JIT) stock control. JIT meant that suppliers delivered enough stock, every working day, to support that day's production. As a result, a car manufacturer no longer had to keep large quantities of stock, and suppliers could also organise production to avoid having to keep large stock quantities ready for delivery.

When stock levels are too high for your normal needs, you tie up cash because the money you pay out for the extra stock will not be translated into cash income until you have used the stock and sold the goods. Excessive stock can result in a bank overdraft to pay suppliers, thereby increasing business costs by the amount of interest paid.

If you do not have specialist software for stock control, you can adapt Microsoft Excel, or similar software, to create a spreadsheet stock control system similar to the hand-written system mentioned above. An advantage is that you can programme the formulas to automatically produce a current balance after every entry.

In addition to managing inventory, you have to control the amounts owed by debtors and to creditors.

CONTROLLING DEBTORS

Unless you operate a purely cash business, the level at which you control your debtors determines the efficiency of your cash income. Most businesses work on a **system of credit** that allows some time before accounts become due for payment. This credit time gives time to use or sell the items purchased and possibly to receive payment for those items before supplier payment is due.

TOP TIPS Most efficient businesses try to balance the credit that they allow to customers with the credit they receive from suppliers which, hopefully, allows time for money to be received from customers before they have to pay supplier accounts as they fall due.

Unfortunately, customers do not always stick to credit terms or pay accounts on time, which can put a business under pressure when suppliers demand that their accounts are paid on time.

Agreeing credit terms with customers

When a customer asks for credit terms, you are likely to be tempted by the vision of the extra business, but you have to remember that unpaid accounts cost you the interest you pay on any money you have to borrow in the face of reduced cash flow.

Therefore, you must find a way of minimising the costs and risks of delayed payments or failed credit customers, and you can consider the following actions:

- Ask the customer for at least two trade references that are suppliers with whom the customer *currently* deals, and are for businesses that supply at least a similar level of credit to the amount you are considering.

- Ask the customer for the name and address of the business's bank, and for written permission to approach the bank for information.

- Contact the trade referees and the customer's bank and ask for their opinions on giving credit to the customer for the amount requested. Make sure that there is no familial relationship between the customer and the trade referees.

- If the trade and bank references are not totally positive, *do not give credit to that customer*. Your business could be at risk if you do so.

- Calculate the effect that credit terms will have on your business cash flow and profits, particularly if you have to increase a bank overdraft.
- If all the factors are positive, write to your customer stating the credit terms you are willing to offer and your *exact* definition of the payment dates that you expect the customer to meet.
- Ask your customer for *written* confirmation that he or she accepts your terms of credit.

TOP TIPS

30-day credit terms can turn out to be much longer if the customer only pays accounts at the end of each month. A delivery made on 2 March might not be paid until the end of April unless you *clearly* state that you expect payment by 2 April – 30 days from delivery.

When you agree credit terms, that does not guarantee that you will receive payment on time and you might have to chase outstanding accounts.

How to control debtor accounts

When you supply your products to a customer, that customer cannot pay the account if you have not issued an invoice. Always make sure that you raise sales invoices either at the time of making the sale or by the end of the trading day.

Some businesses also like to have an account statement, showing the invoices due for payment, and it is a good idea to issue a statement, showing all outstanding invoices to date, at the same time as you submit an invoice.

Keep a record of payments due to you in the form of a debtors' diary, which is really a list of sales invoices sent to customers providing:

- The date on which payment should be made.
- Space for recording 'chasing' activities.

A **debtors' diary** is not a formal accounting record but comprises a list of outstanding invoices kept by the person responsible for ensuring customer payments. You add new sales invoices to the list as they are issued and make notes of any actions you take in relation to any outstanding invoice. This informal record can look something like the following:

Invoice date:	Invoice ref:	Debtor:	Amount:	Date due and chasing details:
March 12	090301	MJ Limited (credit terms 30 days)	~~4589.80~~	Due April 12 Chased April 16 – advised that bank transfer payment will be made April 25 April 26 – bank account checked, amount received
March 12	090302	TSY Limited (credit terms 30 days)	2984.60	Due April 12 Chased April 16 – advised that cheque payment will be made April 30 May 1 - bank account checked, amount not recorded. Chased and advised that all payments were 2 days late and should receive 2 May

Chasing overdue accounts

The debtor's diary shown above suggests a 'standard' practice for chasing overdue accounts. Here are a few more tips on how to chase overdue accounts.

Put aside a specific time each week, perhaps the first hour each Monday morning, to review the debtors' diary list and to telephone any debtor who has not paid on the due date. You might find the following guidelines useful when you telephone a debtor about an overdue account:

- Have a copy of the unpaid invoice in front of you so that you can immediately identify any queries that the customer raises.

- Don't enquire about the goods or services that you delivered to the customer. If he or she has not previously queried the delivery, you do not want to initiate an unwarranted query now.

- Identify the unpaid invoice and amount and ask if payment has been made in the last few days.

- If you receive a negative response from your customer, ask when payment is intended.

- If the stated payment date is acceptable to you, thank the customer and end the call.

- If the stated payment date is unacceptable, ask the customer why he or she is not paying your account within the agreed credit terms. Discuss any reasons given by the customer and explain that you need to receive the payment in order to run your business efficiently. Remind the customer of the payment terms agreed and ask the customer to arrange payment within the next few days.

- Always remain pleasant and *do not lose your temper* even if the customer gets angry. Your customer's anger is a cover for his or her guilt and you are more likely to get support, and keep future business, if you remain calm.
- At the end of the call, always thank the customer for dealing with you positively.

If you doubt the integrity and intention of a customer, you need to be proactive to ensure that you get the outstanding payment, and can apply the following methods:

- Fax or email a copy of the invoice to the customer asking for confirmation that payment will be made by a stated date by which you expect to receive payment.
- If you receive no response, advise the customer or a senior staff member that you or your representative will collect the payment at a specific time on a specific day, giving two or three days' notice.
- Arrange to collect the payment yourself, if possible, so that you can get an impression of the customer's business situation; always telephone before travelling to make sure that a signed cheque is waiting for your collection.
- If the customer still refuses to pay or give a reasonable date for payment, immediately seek the advice of a solicitor, or implement a small claims legal procedure. The sooner you apply legal pressure to this customer, the more likely you are to get paid before other creditors.

TOP TIPS

A customer who refuses to pay your outstanding account is almost certainly failing to pay other accounts. Failing to chase an overdue amount, allowing a customer excessive time to pay, and failing to implement legal action when necessary, can put your business at serious risk of bad debts and failure.

ACTION POINT

What system do you have for controlling debtors and creditors? Do you have a set day each week for chasing overdue accounts? How will you change the system in your business unit to ensure that your debtors and creditors are managed more efficiently?

Although you might find it embarrassing to ask debtors for money, you must keep a strict control on debtor accounts for your own business continuity and safety. Alternatively, you can use a debt collector to collect payment of overdue accounts.

Using a debt collection agency

If you have difficulty obtaining payment for debtor accounts, you might want to consider employing a debt collection agency to work on your behalf. This enables you to avoid the time and embarrassment of chasing customers directly but it comes with disadvantages:

- The agency charges a collection fee, which can be as high as 25% of the invoice value.
- You have no control over the methods used to collect the outstanding amount.
- You have no control over the time it takes to collect an account.
- You can lose a good, though slow-paying, customer as a result of aggressive debt collection.

Invoice discounting and factoring

An alternative to using a debt collection agency can be a process called invoice discounting or factoring.

There are specialist companies in the finance industry that focus on lending money against the value of sales invoices. Invoices do not have to be overdue for payment because the intention is to provide fast cash flow, usually within seven days of the invoice date. This service falls into two distinct, though similar, categories called **invoice discounting** or **factoring**.

Invoice discounting

Companies employing invoice discounting will purchase invoices at a discount from a business. The accepted invoice is paid to the business at a lower, discounted rate representing the fee charged by the finance company. Having purchased an invoice, the finance company is usually responsible for collecting the amount due at the specified date so that the business no longer has to worry about chasing accounts.

Invoice discounting is more appropriate for large, well-known businesses that have high credit-rated customers because the finance company does not want to chase lots of small and slow-paying creditors.

Factoring

Factoring is the process normally available to established businesses and involves a finance company paying a proportion of the value of an invoice quickly, and then collecting payment from the customer on the due date. At this point, the balance of the invoice is paid to the business minus an agreed fee, which is based on the number of days it takes to collect the amount due.

🔍 EXAMPLE

A business decides to factor its invoices and submits an invoice for £10,000 to the finance company on 3 May for payment. The finance company pays 60% of the invoice immediately, less a factoring fee of 10% of invoice value, plus 2% interest per month on outstanding values. The transactions are as follows:

2009		May	June	July
May 3	Invoice submitted	(10,000)		
May 7	60% payment less fee	5,000		
May 7	Factoring fee	(1,000)		
May 31	Interest @ 2%	(120)		
June 23	Interest @ 2%		(120)	
Jun 23	Balance due - account paid		3,760	

The factoring process cost the business £1,240, or 12.4% of invoice value, but the business had access to immediate cash flow of £5,000.

Note how interest is charged on the nominal amount paid to the business rather than the net amount after deduction of charges. Also, if an invoice remains unpaid after a certain length of time, usually 60 days, the amount of the invoice is deducted from any future factored invoices and the business becomes responsible for collecting what is now an entrenched debt.

CONTROLLING CREDITORS

You might wonder why we suggest that you have to control your creditors – surely it is up to suppliers to chase their own accounts. Irresponsible managers sometimes consider that delaying payment of supplier's accounts enables them to keep money back and reduce their risk of cash shortages, or perhaps gain a little extra interest. Failing to pay accounts on time risks losing a sound trading reputation and reduces the opportunity to negotiate credit terms with other suppliers and overdrafts with a bank. No-one wants to deal with a bad payer.

However, there are other operational reasons for paying supplier accounts on time, which include the following:

- An unpaid supplier can refuse to deliver more supplies that you need to run your business, resulting in business operations being interrupted and preventing you from meeting your customers' needs.
- A supplier who is not paid on time might not be able to continue in business and might have to close down, resulting in you having to find another supplier who might be less efficient and more expensive.

It is not worth creating problems for your supplier and yourself by paying accounts late; it is far better to manage your cash flow so that you can pay accounts on time and protect your reputation and your supply chain.

You manage your creditor accounts in a similar way to the debtor process shown above, through a **creditors' diary** or **aged creditor analysis** if you have a computer accounting system.

We can now look at cash flow management.

MANAGING CASH FLOW

Cash flow is the daily process covering:

- Cash flowing into your business from product sales and any other sources of income.
- Cash flowing out from your business to pay creditors and loans or to purchase capital assets.
- The difference between inflow and outflow, which creates a surplus for your business unit, or results in a shortage of cash to keep the business operating.

We mentioned the purchase of capital assets above as part of cash flow. However, most businesses deal with capital expenditure as a non-operational part of the business, separately from normal operating cash flow. This chapter deals with cash flow from a normal operating point of view.

The seasonalised budget for 2010 produced by StoneGlass showed that the business gradually builds up monthly profits until June when income is reduced because of the annual close-down period, yet fixed costs, holiday pay and maintenance costs still have to be paid. At that point the profit becomes a loss, though it recovers again once the business starts up in August. However, the budget does not reflect the probable cash flowing through the business because it shows when products are produced and sold, and when costs are created but does not show when cash is received from customers or when suppliers' accounts are paid.

ACTION POINT

Do you work out, *in advance*, the pattern of cash coming into and out from your business unit for at least the next month? Do you get caught out by not having enough cash to pay accounts at the end of a month? Are there certain times of year when you have a cash shortfall? What do you do about any cash shortfall problems? How do they impact on your business operation?

In order to identify, in advance, the potential impacts of cash flow on your business unit, you have to prepare a **cash flow forecast** that predicts the likely financial transactions, at the point of payment, for a given future period, normally the next one or two months.

Creating a cash flow forecast

In format, a cash flow forecast is very similar to a budget statement though it tries to show:

- The dates on which money is likely to be received by the business.
- The dates when money has to be paid out by the business.

You will probably be able to produce a cash flow forecast only for the next month or two because most businesses use 30-day credit facilities and you may not be able to predict your actual sales income and the effect of credit arrangements for more than two months in advance. This is the case for StoneGlass, which uses 30-day credit terms for both customers and major suppliers.

Q CASE STUDY

StoneGlass produced the following budget statement for January and February of 2010:

	Year	Jan	Feb
Days:	234	20	20
Turnover	4,300,000	367,521	367,521
Direct costs:			
Materials	2,310,000	197,436	197,436
Wages	850,000	72,650	72,650
Employee costs	57,000	4,872	4,872
Maintenance	8,000		
Depreciation	73,500	6,282	6,282
Electricity	18,000	1,538	1,538
Water	2,000	171	171
Consumables	4,000	342	342
Packaging costs	12,000	1,026	1,026
Business rates	22,000	1,833	1,833
Insurance	15,000	15,000	
Total direct costs	3,371,500	301,150	286,150
Gross profit	928,500	66,372	81,372
Overheads:			
Owners salaries	200,000	16,667	16,667

Admin salaries	90,000	7,500	7,500
Employee costs	30,000	2,500	2,500
Design costs	80,000	6,838	6,838
Marketing	10,000	855	855
Stationery	3,000	256	256
Telephone & post	8,000	684	684
Maintenance	2,000	0	
Employee consumables	1,000	85	85
Loan interest	80,000	6,667	6,667
Audit	7,000	0	
Bank charges	5,000	427	427
Total overheads	516,000	42,479	42,479
Net profit before tax	412,500	23,893	38,893

However, the family knew that:
- Customers would not pay accounts within the month of invoicing.
- On average, customers always took up to 60 days to pay accounts.
- Supplier accounts were often delayed for up to 60 days because of the failure to get customer payments on time.

After the bank withdrew the overdraft facility, the Stone family knew that it had to identify cash flow problems in advance, and produced the following cash flow prediction from the above budget:

	Jan Budget	Jan Cash flow	Feb Cash flow	March Cash flow
Turnover	367,521			
Total cash inflow				367,521
Direct costs:				
Materials	197,436			197,436
Wages	72,650	72,650		
Employee costs	4,872	4,872		
Maintenance				

Depreciation	6,282			
Electricity	1,538		1,538	
Water	171		171	
Consumables	342	342		
Packaging costs	1,026		1,026	
Business rates	1,833		1,833	
Insurance	15,000	15,000		
Overheads:				
Owners salaries	16,667	16,667		
Admin salaries	7,500	7,500		
Employee costs	2,500	2,500		
Design costs	6,838	3,438	3,400	
Marketing	855	855		
Stationery	256	256		
Telephone & post	684		684	
Maintenance	0			
Employee consumables	85	85		
Loan interest	6,667	6,667		
Audit	0			
Bank charges	427	427		
Total cash outflow	343,629	131,259	8,652	197,436
Net cash flow for month	23,892	-131,259	-8,652	170,085
Cash balance brought forward on first day of month	103,900	103,900	32,641	23,989
Cash balance carried forward on last day of month	127,792	-27,359	23,989	194,074

Notes:

- *Depreciation was excluded from the cash flow statement because it is an accounting transaction and not a cash transaction.*
- *Cash brought forward on 1 January (and into February) is the net cash flow balance at the end of December 2009.*

This cash flow statement now shows that while StoneGlass expected to have a positive cash flow in January according to the budget, in reality the credit arrangements meant that January cash flow would produce a shortfall of £27,359 which, in the absence of a bank overdraft, the family would have to find a way of financing.

You can now see the effect that credit arrangements can have on the cash flow of a business and why you have to make sure that you collect payments from debtors according to the credit terms agreed. You should also now understand why it is so important to create a cash flow prediction for your business to avoid being unknowingly left short of cash to pay accounts, and to pay any loan and interest instalments as they fall due – failing to pay loan instalments can put your collateral at risk.

ACTION POINT

Do you have credit agreements with your customers and major suppliers? How long, on average, does it take your customers to pay their accounts? Do you pay your suppliers on time? What effect do these credit agreements have on your cash flow? Are you ever 'caught short'?

QUICK RECAP

- *You can have a profitable business yet still fail because of poor cash flow.*
- *In order to manage cash flow, you have to manage your working capital.*
- *Stocks need to be maintained at an optimum level commensurate with the business unit's level of operation.*
- *Credit arrangements can destroy your business if they are not managed efficiently.*
- *Make sure that customers pay accounts on time by assertively chasing overdue accounts.*
- *A non-paying customer is not an asset to your business – it is a liability that can become a disaster.*
- *Pay suppliers on time to protect necessary deliveries to your business and to ensure that you have good suppliers in the future.*
- *A cash flow statement predicts positive or negative cash balances.*
- *You can choose – create a cash flow statement or organise an overdraft – just remember that the overdraft costs you money and profit!*

CHAPTER 6

Capital expenditure and managing capital resources

You might have wondered why we have omitted to talk about managing capital assets, which cost a great deal of money and can have a dramatic impact on your cash resources. It is precisely because of the high cost of capital assets that we have isolated them into a chapter of their own.

In this chapter, we will look at:

• How you assess capital expenditure.
• Controlling capital assets over their lifetimes.

WHAT ARE CAPITAL ASSETS?

The type of capital assets you use in your business will depend on the type of business you operate, though the following assets will apply to most businesses:

- Premises.
- Machinery and equipment for manufacturing and packaging.
- Equipment for moving heavy materials, such as a fork-lift truck.
- Vehicles for delivering products to customers.
- Furniture on which to assemble and pack products.
- Furniture and equipment used in an office.
- Shelves or shop furniture on which to display products for sale.
- Shelves or other fixtures on which to store materials and stock.

Many businesses choose to rent or lease capital assets to avoid the heavy expenditures involved. This is a perfectly reasonable option though there are leasing costs that can be higher than the interest costs of a business loan. In this chapter, we deal with capital assets that are purchased and owned by the business.

ACTION POINT

Think about the fixed assets with which you operate your business. How do you assess the current value of capital assets? How do you know where your major assets are located? What records of capital assets do you keep?

Always make sure that any fixed assets that you buy have sufficient capacity to meet your business needs for the foreseeable future, and certainly for the next three to five years.

THE REAL COST OF PURCHASING FIXED ASSETS

When you buy fixed assets, you tie up money for a number of years. In large organisations, senior managers often have to deal with requests from several business units for money to buy new equipment; if the capital investment fund is limited, they may have to decide which investment is most advantageous for the group as a whole.

TOP TIPS

The process of capital expenditure is sometimes referred to by financial specialists as CAPEX. When business unit managers have to compete with each other to get the funds for capital investment, they are said to be 'competing for scarce resources'.

Since cash is always a scarce resource, you have to appraise the potential benefits and effects of an investment decision using one of the established investment appraisal techniques, such as:

- Payback value: which looks at the total cost of the money invested.
- Internal rate of return: which considers the return that you should get from a capital investment.
- Net present value: which calculates the total cost of the investment and the true value obtained from that investment.

Before making an investment decision, you want to be sure that you have an acceptable payback value.

CALCULATING THE PAYBACK VALUE OF AN INVESTMENT

This is the process that StoneGlass implemented for 2010.

Q CASE STUDY

StoneGlass knew that it had to purchase new equipment and negotiated a loan of £1m, repayable over 10 years at an interest rate of 8% per annum calculated on the balance outstanding at the beginning of each year. The interest schedule was calculated as follows:

			8% pa
Loan		1,000,000	80,000
Year 2	100,000	900,000	72,000
Year 3	100,000	800,000	64,000
Year 4	100,000	700,000	56,000
Year 5	100,000	600,000	48,000
Year 6	100,000	500,000	40,000
Year 7	100,000	400,000	32,000
Year 8	100,000	300,000	24,000
Year 9	100,000	200,000	16,000
Year 10	100,000	100,000	8,000
Year 11	100,000	0	0
	1,000,000		440,000

In order to make the investment decision worthwhile, by covering the costs involved, the investment would have to pay back at least £440,000 over the 10 year period. Looking at the flexed budget that prompted the investment decision, it was clear that:

- *Without the capital investment, the business expected to produce a profit before tax of £64,170.*
- *With the new capital assets, the business expected to produce a profit before tax of £412,500 in 2010.*
- *Therefore, the new capital equipment should provide a payback value per annum, which was more than enough to cover the interest cost each year.*

When you calculate a payback value, you might want to also take into account other hidden costs or profit opportunities that you have to forego in order to make the investment. These costs are usually referred to as opportunity costs.

Opportunity costs

Opportunity costs are costs that arise when you choose one alternative investment over other opportunities that are available at the time.

🔍 EXAMPLE

A large corporation with a number of investment projects will calculate payback values before choosing the investment that provides the best long-term value for the corporation. In other words, it might choose a project with a lower payback value because it provides broader opportunities in the long-term. Having made this choice, the business will have lost the opportunity to achieve a higher short-term payback value, which is the opportunity cost it has foregone in the investment decision. In this case, the payback calculation should include this opportunity cost to provide a realistic assessment of the cost to the business over its expected lifetime. Senior management say, 'Because we have chosen to invest in Project C, we have lost the opportunity to achieve extra profits from Project A, so we want the payback from Project C to cover the opportunity costs we have lost'.

In some ways, the calculation of payback value is a statement of the obvious, and it is usual to calculate payback in a more formalistic way, called the accounting rate of return.

Calculating the accounting rate of return on an investment

The accounting rate of return assesses a capital project's financial benefit to the business by comparing average net profit from the project with the original investment cost. As a formula, this appears as:

$$\frac{\text{Average annual net profit} \times 100}{\text{Investment cost}}$$

Let's look at how StoneGlass applies this calculation.

Q CASE STUDY

In the calculation above, StoneGlass assumed that the £1m loan produced an extra annual profit of £348,330 for 10 years. However, the 10 years reflected the projected lifetime of the new capital assets that were purchased for £635,000 and the £375,000 balance of the loan was used for working capital. Therefore, it was the capital investment of £635,000 that produced the payback calculated. Using this information, StoneGlass calculated the accounting rate of return on the investment as follows:

		£
	Lifetime profit – 10 years @ £348,330	3,483,300
Less:	Investment cost	635,000
	Profit from investment	2,848,300
	Investment profit per annum	284,830

$$\frac{\text{Average net profit pa} \times 100}{\text{Investment cost}} = \frac{£284,830 \times 100}{£635,000} = 44.85\%$$

Therefore, StoneGlass's accounting rate of return on this investment is 44.85% per annum.

The accounting rate of return is sometimes referred to as the internal rate of return.

TOP TIPS

This calculation highlights the percentage return or profit margin achieved from a particular capital investment on the basis that:

- The level of profit will remain the same for future years.
- There is an assumed capital asset lifetime (in StoneGlass's case 10 years) which could turn out to be longer or shorter.
- There is no residual value remaining for the capital asset at the end of the assumed lifetime period.
- The value of money remains the same for future years.

TOP TIPS

The effect of the falling value of money over a number of years is referred to by accounting professionals and economists as the time value of money, but is generally referred to as inflation.

These assumptions are very broad, and while we cannot foresee the lifetime or residual value of the asset we can try to make some allowance for the fall in the value of money during future years. We do this by calculating an outcome called **net present value**.

Calculating net present value (NPV)

When we calculate the impact of long-term investments, we have to take into account that future income will not have the same value as the same amount of money received today, because inflation will have eroded some of its value. This means that you need to allow for inflation when assessing large and long-term investments.

We calculate the effects of inflation through a process called **discounted cash flow**, which seeks to identify future value by multiplying the present value by an inflation index, sometimes called the retail price index (RPI) or consumer price index (CPI) issued and updated as Government statistics.

HOW TO CALCULATE DISCOUNTED CASH FLOWS

When you calculate discounted cash flows, you should obtain current CPI values from the Government statistics website or from similar published data. This data has a base year against which other years (or perhaps months) are indexed. In other words, a CPI table shows that while £1 was the base value at one date, its value subsequently fell to the lower value shown. The Chancellor of the Exchequer uses CPI data to forecast the predicted movement in inflation for future years.

At the time that this book was written, Alistair Darling, Chancellor of the Exchequer, announced that he expected inflation to remain a little above 2% for 2010.

In order to demonstrate the effects of inflation, let us take an example.

🔍 EXAMPLE

A small business was advised that a franchise that would cost £45,000 to buy would produce a profit before tax of £15,000 per annum. Having researched and calculated the expected inflation index for the next five years, the owner found that inflation was expected to increase by 5% per annum; he calculated a predicted future index as follows:

$$\frac{\text{Current value}}{1 = \text{Inflation rate}} = \text{Inflated value} = \frac{£1.00}{1.05} = £0.95$$

The predicted inflation index and predicted profit values for the next five years were now as follows:

Year:	Profit £	Index:	Value £
2010	15,000	1	15,000
2011	15,000	0.95	14,250
2012	15,000	0.91	13,650
2013	15,000	0.86	12,040
2014	15,000	0.82	12,300
2015	15,000	0.78	11,700

The owner was able to calculate that, within five years, the stated profit of £15,000 would only be worth £11,700.

The Stone family after carrying out a similar calculation realised that they were spending money now to achieve a predicted profit whose value would actually be worth less in the future. Therefore they needed a way to calculate how inflation would impact on their investment. They turned to the process for calculating **net present value** (NPV).

How to apply the NPV calculation

Net present value (NPV) is a process that includes inflation in order to *fairly* compare the real value of future incomes with the present value of money spent, and assumes that income and expenditure are calculated at the end of each year of operation.

Q CASE STUDY

Taking the investment of £635,000 and the predicted future profit of £348,330 per annum, StoneGlass assumed an inflation rate of 5% per annum for the next 10 years. NPV was then calculated as follows:

Year:	Cost (£):	Profits £	Net Cash Flow £	Inflation Index:	Present Value £
2010	(635,000)		(635,000)	1	-635,000
2010		348,330		1	348,330
2011		348,330		0.95	330,914
2012		348,330		0.91	316,980
2013		348,330		0.86	299,564
2014		348,330		0.82	285,631
2015		348,330		0.78	271,697
2016		348,330		0.74	257,764
2017		348,330		0.71	247,314
2018		348,330		0.67	233,381
2019		348,330		0.64	222,931
NPV					2,179,506

In other words, the investment will create a profit of £2,179,506 over 10 years, after taking inflation into account. This is an average annual profit of £217,950, which is a little over 60% of the profit expected on a 'current value' basis.

TOP TIPS If an investment is made, or equipment is eventually sold, part way through a trading year, you have to apportion income or sales values for the months of operation only, rather than for the full trading year. If an asset is sold, that sale value is shown as income in the year of sale and calculated accordingly.

ACTION POINT

This would be a good point at which to stop and calculate the impact of inflation on any capital expenditure in your business. If possible, try to get hold of actual CPI data for the period over which you complete the calculation and/or estimate reasonable future data on the basis of Government announcements. If your NPV results in a negative value, it will mean that the investment return (including inflation) does not justify the money being spent.

Clearly, a large organisation uses the above calculations to show which investment is likely be the most cost efficient in terms of the inflation-proofed return achieved. However, a very small business owner might have to buy required equipment irrespective of its NPV. You have to decide how you can best use these accounting tools in your business. Once you have made your decision and purchased capital assets, you have to make sure that those assets are managed efficiently.

MANAGING THE CAPITAL ASSETS IN YOUR BUSINESS

When you spend a large amount of money on an asset you are naturally inclined to look after that asset and to occasionally assess its value to you and perhaps to others who may be interested in buying it when you choose to sell.

When you purchase a car or a house you understand that you will have to invest in materials and maintenance to protect its integrity and value. Most owners keep an eye on the marketplace value of their assets.

Provide the expected asset value to your business by:
• Buying the correct materials to ensure optimum efficiency and productivity.

- Protecting an asset's integrity and viability by correct maintenance procedures.
- Ensuring maximum production capability by carrying out regular maintenance.
- Allowing for the loss of value over time.
- Calculating an asset's business value at the end of every year.

Most businesses manage capital assets through a document called a fixed asset register.

Keeping a fixed asset register

A fixed asset register usually includes the following:
- Description of the asset, including any registration numbers.
- Supplier name, address and contact details (to arrange repairs and spares).
- Cost at date of purchase.
- Costs of installing and commissioning asset ready for production.
- Details and costs of major renovation and upgrading processes.
- Rate and cost of annual depreciation.
- Price for which the asset is sold at the end of its useful life.

In a fixed asset register, each asset is recorded on its own single page, which looks something like that shown opposite.

ACTION POINT

Do you have information for each of your capital assets, such as model number, registration number and supplier details? Would this be a good time to start a fixed asset register to give you a record of each of the capital assets used in your business?

Q CASE STUDY

When StoneGlass purchased its first glass forming machine in 2003 for £100,000, it recorded the purchase in a fixed asset register as follows:

Supplier: Glassform Engineering Ltd. Roundabout Industrial Park, Birmingham, B1 9ZZ. Tel: 0121 987 6543. Fax: 0121 987 6542				
Details:	Date:	Cost (£):	Depreciation:	Value (£):
Purchase cost	01.01.03	100,000		
Installation cost	02.01.03	0		
Commissioned	02.01.03	100,000		100,000
	31.12.03		10,000	90,000
	31.12.04		10,000	80,000
	31.12.05		10,000	70,000
	31.12.06		10,000	60,000
	31.12.07		10,000	50,000
	31.12.08		10,000	40,000
	31.12.09		10,000	30,000
	31.12.10		10,000	20,000
	31.12.12		10,000	10,000
	31.12.13		10,000	0

Although this shows that StoneGlass calculated annual depreciation valuations for the estimated life period of the asset, in reality it would calculate annual depreciation and update the asset register each year. If the asset is refurbished and the value increased the cost of the upgrade is added to the fixed asset register.

Note that you do not record normal maintenance costs implemented to keep the asset operating efficiently, because normal maintenance does not add value to the asset. However, you can file additional information in the fixed asset register, such as:

- The original purchase invoice to provide full information about asset purchase.
- Technical information about an upgrade to identify how the asset has been improved.
- Details of maintenance to provide a 'service history' for an eventual purchaser.

Since the fixed asset register represents the life history of a capital asset, it is appropriate that the 'death', disposal or sale of an asset from the business should be recorded to complete the asset's history in the business.

Disposing of a capital asset

When you dispose of an asset, you have to:

- Record the disposal in the fixed asset register.
- Record the amount received from the sale.
- Calculate the profit or loss resulting from the sale, taking into account the depreciation already calculated.

When you sell a capital asset for more than the value currently shown in the fixed asset register, the business receives a profit which must be shown as an additional business income in financial accounts for that trading year. If you dispose of a capital asset at a value lower than the value currently in the fixed asset register, you can claim a 'loss' in your financial accounts for that trading year.

If we assume that StoneGlass decided to sell the old machine in 2011, we can see the effect of the sale in the fixed asset register.

Q CASE STUDY

During 2011, StoneGlass realised that the old glass forming machine was no longer useable and decided to sell it at auction on 30 June 2011. On 1 July 2011 the business received a cheque from the auctioneers for £4,300, which was entered into the fixed asset register.

Details:	Date:	Cost (£):	Depreciation:	Value (£):
Supplier: Glassform Engineering Ltd. Roundabout Industrial Park, Birmingham, B1 9ZZ. Tel: 0121 987 6543. Fax: 0121 987 6542				
Purchase cost	01.01.03	100,000		
Installation cost	02.01.03	0		
Commissioned	02.01.03	100,000		100,000
Depreciation	31.12.03		10,000	90,000
Depreciation	31.12.04		10,000	80,000
Depreciation	31.12.05		10,000	70,000
Depreciation	31.12.06		10,000	60,000
Depreciation	31.12.07		10,000	50,000
Depreciation	31.12.08		10,000	40,000
Depreciation	31.12.09		10,000	30,000
Depreciation	31.12.10		10,000	20,000
Depreciation	30.06.11		5,000	15,000
Disposal	01.07.11	(4,500)		10,500
Book value	01.07.11			0
Loss on sale				10,500

StoneGlass completed the asset page in the fixed asset register by:
- *Calculating the depreciation allowance to the point of disposal (30 June 2011), and the value before disposal as £15,000.*
- *Showing the amount of £4,500 received for the asset.*
- *Determining the loss on the asset of £10,500.*

In the end-of-year accounts, StoneGlass included £5,000 in its depreciation costs, £4,500 as additional income and reduced its total fixed assets value by £20,000.

ACTION POINT

Study the above case study carefully to make sure that you understand why the sale of the asset has been recorded as shown. Check the calculations and make sure that you understand how the 'book' profit of £20,000 at the end of 2010 has been dealt with, in terms of depreciation and value received as a result of the sale.

QUICK RECAP

- *You can calculate the value return from capital asset expenditure by calculating the payback value of the investment.*
- *The internal rate of return on an investment compares average net profit with the cost of the investment.*
- *A net present value calculation tells you the real return of an investment taking into account inflation.*
- *To identify the effects of inflation, you can calculate discounted cash flow using an index such as the CPI.*
- *Capital assets can be managed using a fixed asset register in which you record purchase costs, upgrading costs, annual depreciation and any value received when the asset is eventually sold.*

CHAPTER 7

Understanding final accounts

Dealing with parts of accounts in isolation, as we have done in earlier chapters, can become confusing and this is probably a good time to bring fragmented knowledge together to help you to understand business accounts and to be able to 'read' the meanings of different aspects of those accounts. In this chapter we will help you to get a better understanding from any P&L and balance sheet that you look at in the future.

GETTING TO FINAL ACCOUNTS

TOP TIPS

The phrase 'final accounts' refers to the accounts that are 'finalised' at the end of each year and which culminate in the **profit and loss account** and the **balance sheet**.

During a trading year, source documents such as sales and purchase invoices are recorded daily or weekly in the accounting records of the business. At the end of each trading month, accounting records are totalled to provide totals for the trading month for:

- Income (total sales invoices).
- Costs of production, or cost of sales (total direct costs).
- Costs of administration (total overheads).
- Costs of financing (banking, loan and interest repayments and financial services).

Account totals are summarised into a financial statement called a **trial balance** prepared by the finance department. Using the trial balance, accounting specialists prepare one of the following:

- Monthly management accounts.
- Final accounts for a full trading year.

Every business has to legally state its 'normal' trading year, or period of 12 calendar months. However, a business can change its declared trading year, which can involve a one-off trading period that is longer or shorter than a 12 month period.

Q CASE STUDY

StoneGlass's original trading year was from 1 April in one year to 31 March in the following year. Because Easter, when annual accounts had to be prepared, was a busy time for sales and production period, the business's financial year was changed to 1 January to 31 December and StoneGlass Limited produced the following 'annual' accounts:

- *Final accounts for the 9-month period from 1 April 2000 to 31 December 2000*
- *Final accounts for the 1-year period 1 January to 31 December 2001*

This brought accounts 'into line' with the new business year.

Management accounts consist of a profit and loss account only for a one-month trading period. Final accounts, for a one-year trading period, consist of both a profit and loss account and a Balance Sheet.

When totals are brought together to create a profit and loss account and a balance sheet, the end results can appear to be a confusing mass of numbers and other information. However, these accounts are based on standard or common formats that enable you to quickly identify information about the business.

LOOKING AT A PROFIT AND LOSS ACCOUNT (P&L)

Profit and loss accounts can be formatted in different ways in order to demonstrate specific areas of the accounts, though all P&Ls contain the same contents in terms of income and expenditure. Notice how we have presented the information below more formally than in previous chapters in order to highlight the totals of various sections by enclosing the contents of totals in heavily-lined boxes.

TOP TIPS

It is normal practice to always provide, for comparison, final accounts for the current year and the previous year. This enables you to immediately recognise if the business has grown or changed significantly during the trading year.

Q CASE STUDY

Early in 2010, StoneGlass published the following P&L for the 2009 trading year:

P&L ACCOUNT FOR STONEGLASS LIMITED for the year from 1 January to 31 December 2009					
		2008	2008	2009	2009
Turnover	1		2,870,000		3,480,000
Cost of sales:					
Materials		1,560,000		2,198,000	
Wages	2	548,500		796,000	
Employee costs		31,000		54,800	
Maintenance		16,300		23,600	
Depreciation	3	10,000		10,000	
Electricity		13,700		18,100	
Water		2,800		3,800	
Consumables		5,100		8,300	
Packaging costs		6,900		8,700	
Business rates		16,000		18,600	
Insurance		11,600		13,400	
Total direct costs			2,221,900		3,153,300
Gross profit			648,100		326,700

Overheads:					
Owners salaries	4	150,000		180,000	
Admin salaries	5	53,000		82,400	
Employee costs		14,000		27,400	
Design costs					
Marketing		6,800		8,100	
Stationery		700		3,400	
Telephone & post		5,900		7,600	
Maintenance		600		1,700	
Empl. consumables		900		2,300	
Loan interest		0		0	
Audit		4,600		6,100	
Bank charges		3,300		4,700	
Total overheads			239,800		323,700
Net profit before tax			408,300		3,000
Less: Tax	6		170,000		4,000
Retained profit			238,300		-1,000

Notes to the accounts:
1. *Turnover represented income from sale of products only; the business received no income from other sources.*
2. *Employee wages includes amounts contributed by the business to employees' personal pension schemes.*
3. *Depreciation is calculated on a straight-line basis for all fixed assets.*
4. *Owners' salaries includes amounts contributed by the business to personal pension schemes, amounting to 5% of salaries.*
5. *Admin salaries includes amounts contributed by the business to employees' personal pension schemes.*
6. *Tax payable has been calculated at the current business rate and the amount reserved for payment to HM Customs and Excise.*

Companies include numbered notes to allow more extensive information to be provided in 'notes to the accounts'. For example, Note 1 tells you that turnover represented sales of products only and excluded sale of fixed assets.

Using information shown in a P&L, you can quickly determine the:

- Total income of the business.
- Cost of sales (direct costs) of producing that income.
- Cost of administration.
- Value of profit retained in the business.

You can then compare business performance year by year, and you can compare your business performance with that of competitors for which you can obtain accounts. These comparisons tell you how efficiently you are managing your business finances and highlight differences between you and your competitors. We show you how to carry out objective comparisons in the next chapter.

> **TOP TIPS**
>
> A P&L covers a trading period described as 'the year from 1 January to 31 December 2009'. A balance sheet shows values at a specific date, usually the last date of the trading year shown in a P&L; the heading indicates the date of valuation as 'at 31 December 2009'.

Some types of business separate trading costs into slightly different categories to identify major cost areas, such as:

- Operating costs (instead of direct costs or cost of sales).
- Marketing costs.
- Administration costs.
- Financial and legal costs.

A business that sells its products directly to consumers through leaflet mailings or magazine advertisements has major cost items associated with the marketing process. In this case, the business will probably have a separate section in the P&L to cover 'marketing costs'.

A business that renovates properties has significant legal costs associated with buying and selling and associated loans. In this case, it can show legal and financing costs in a separate section of the P&L.

When you look at a P&L, check to see how costs are formatted so that you understand and can identify the basic pattern of the account, which shows:

• How much the business has generated in income.
• How much it has cost to produce that income.
• How much profit it has made.

ACTION POINT

Get hold of the accounts for one or more of your competitors and, for a specific trading year, list the totals for income, direct costs, overheads and profit before tax. Next to each total, list the similar values for your business for the same (or nearest) trading period. How do the totals compare? Are you more or less efficient at controlling your direct costs and overheads? How does your level of profitability compare with your competitors'? If your competitor is more efficient than you, how can you reverse that factor?

LOOKING AT A BALANCE SHEET (BS)

Having provided detailed information in the P&L on the performance of the business during a trading year, a company seeks to show the value of the business at the end of that trading period through its balance sheet (BS).

Q CASE STUDY

StoneGlass published the following Balance Sheet for the 2009 trading year:

BALANCE SHEET FOR STONEGLASS LIMITED as at 31 December 2009		2008	2008	2009	2009
Fixed assets:	7		290,000		275,000
Premises		200,000		200,000	
Machinery		70,000		60,000	
Office		20,000		15,000	
Current assets:			877,700		1,064,300
Inventory		380,000		492,000	
Debtors		497,700		572,300	
Cash at bank		0		0	
Current liabilities:			605,000		777,600
Creditors		392,000		528,600	
Bank overdraft		213,000		249,000	
Long-term liabilities:			0		0
Loan		0		0	
Net assets			562,700		561,700
Equity:			562,700		561,700
Owners investment		50,000		50,000	
Retained profits		512,700		511,700	

Notes to the accounts:

7. *Fixed assets are shown at their current valuation in the company's books after the deduction of depreciation. Annual depreciation is as follows:*

Asset:	Book value c/fwd	Depreciation for year	Value shown in BS
Premises	200,000	0	200,000
Machinery	70,000	10,000	60,000
Office	20,000	5,000	15,000

You know from the P&L how well the business has generated sales, produced products and paid for its administration; you now want to know, from the BS, how that period of trading has added value to the business.

A balance sheet is separated into sections to identify facilities of specific characteristics that create the following groups:
• Fixed assets.
• Current assets.
• Current liabilities.
• Long-term liabilities (for repayment after one year).
• Owners' equity invested and retained in the business.
The values shown by these sections tell you about the following:
• Movements in the value of fixed assets, which identify if the business has acquired new assets, sold assets or continues to depreciate existing assets.
• The relationship between current assets and current liabilities, which confirms that the business can pay current (immediately payable) debts from its current assets.
• Movements in the amount of cash available in the business bank account or an overdraft.
• Changes in long-term debt, which tell you if the business is borrowing more money or repaying existing long-term loans.
• The proportion of profits being retained in the business for future expansion.
When you look for the above information in competitors' accounts, these are particular issues to look for in the account tables or in associated notes.

Fixed assets are sometimes shown in a BS as a total value, which is analysed as a note to the account. Fixed assets can include expensive executive cars that are not productive to the business - £500,000 of production machinery means a lot more in a business than £500,000 of luxury executive cars, though some businesses see posh cars as an 'indication of success'.

Current assets include inventory that does not produce cash for the business until it is converted to sales income; therefore, it is not readily available to pay creditors.

A static bank overdraft, particularly during a time of economic downturn, can indicate a business under financial pressure from its bank manager who wants to see the overdraft moving between positive and negative values through any trading period.

Profit retention usually means that owners intend to grow the business.

The ability to identify sections of a BS and understand their meaning gives you an understanding of the business you are looking at. Separating individual values from the melee of information helps you to deal with different aspects of the business in small and understandable chunks.

ACTION POINT

Obtain the accounts for one or more competitors and, for a specific trading year, list the totals for fixed assets, current assets, current liabilities, long-term liabilities and equity. Next to each total, list the similar values for your business for the same (or nearest) trading period. How do the totals compare? Are you using more fixed assets to produce your sales income? Are you more or less efficient at controlling your debtors and creditors? Do you keep higher or lower stock levels than your competitors? Do you have larger long-term loans than your competitors? How does your level of equity compare with your competitors? If a competitor is more efficient than you are, how can you reverse that factor?

Comparisons of values between your business and a competitor are straightforward and give you an immediate way of checking your performance against that of another business. However, you should also be checking your current performance against your past results to see if you are becoming more or less efficient as you gain more and more expertise in your industry sector. In the next chapter, we will demonstrate the tools you can use to continually analyse financial management performance and efficiency.

LOOKING AT LARGE CORPORATE ACCOUNTS

TOP TIPS

Large organisations and corporations are legally required to publish detailed annual accounting information, which is usually contained in a booklet called the Annual Report and Accounts. You can ask for a copy from any company listed on the London Stock Exchange, or you can access the information from websites. You can also obtain a copy of the accounts of any non-listed company from Companies House, though you will have to pay the copying fee involved.

Large public company or corporate accounts will follow the traditional formats described above, but the volume of information that must be legally included in the accounts makes them appear chaotic and confusing. When you look at these accounts, you should isolate specific issues and values in which you are interested and then access any notes that provide associated information for that item. This enables you to 'simplify' your analyses.

The additional information provided in corporate accounts is also enhanced by:
• Account 'highlights'.
• Executive reports.

Account highlights

Many large corporations start a report and accounts with 'Highlights', which are a summary of what the company considers to be the most important aspects of business performance. This summary is intended to provide at-a-glance data for those who do not want to sift through the detailed information provided. Highlighted data must always be accurate, but can be presented in a way that takes the eye away from an element that hasn't performed too well.

🔍 EXAMPLE

Highlighted information might show the following data:

	2008	2009
	£000s	£000s
Total income	2,137	2,498
Profit before tax	247	259

As intended, this data provides at-a-glance confidence that the business is performing well and increasing its sales and profit performance. However, the data provided could hide the fact that the business lost a considerable amount of market share in 2009 and sold off fixed assets for £550,000 which it has included in the values shown. This additional information must legally be included in the formal accounts that appear later in the publication but the highlights hide the actual performance of the normal business operation which should have appeared as follows:

	2008	2009
	£000s	£000s
Total income	2,137	1,948
Profit before tax	247	(- 291)

Executive reports

A published report and accounts usually contains a Chairperson's Report and/or a Chief Executive's Report, which follows quickly after financial highlights to provide an overview of the year's performance and predictions for the next year. This information must be accurate and substantiated by the information in the accounts, but words can be written in ways to 'change the colour' of the information given, possibly making poor results sound more positive.

When reading these statements, try to read 'between the lines' so as to get the feel of what is *really* meant by the content. Executives' reports have one objective - to maintain the confidence of shareholders and encourage others to become shareholders, so they usually promote more successful aspects of the business. Therefore, look at the trends in the actual numbers rather than just accept information provided by the highlights and executive reports.

Q EXAMPLE

A Chairman's Report might contain the statement, 'Last year saw us successfully defending the market for our traditional products and we are confident that we can use our long experience in this marketplace to fight the challenge to our normal uplifts.'

In reality, the Chairman might be saying, 'Our past-accepted products have become outdated and are being threatened by new products entering the marketplace. We could find our profitability under pressure in the coming years as a result of these market changes.'

Beware of any graphics used in corporate accounts because graphs, tables, bar charts, pie charts and pictograms (pictures representing different values) can be used to mislead you. Graphics highlight the issues that the company wants you to focus on but the lack of real values can distract you from problem areas.

Accessing information through notes to the accounts

Notes to the accounts provide more extensive information such as the names, ages and experience of all directors, though the information can cover up horror stories about how excessive executive bonuses are awarded.

Corporations have executive directors who work full-time in the business plus a number of non-executive directors who attend board meetings to add their experience to decision making. Non-executive directors (NEDs) are nominated and appointed by executive directors. The appointment of NEDs to various banks has raised questions since it has become clear that not all have the knowledge and experience required for a major banking corporation. The number of NED positions held by one individual can prevent him or her from applying sufficient time to their responsibilities for any sponsoring companies, especially when they are an executive director of another company. It appears that the NED 'circuit' results in NED positions in an industry being 'shared out' between a small group of individuals who receive substantial additional fees from the 'circuit'. There is now a question whether some NEDs are 'fit for purpose' and if they are strong enough, when necessary, to vote against the executive directors who appoint them and who pay NED fees every month!

Another question raised about NEDs is that they are often responsible for implementing executive remuneration, which can include salary, bonus and pension contributions. It takes a very strong NED to tell an executive director that he has not performed and will not get a salary increase or bonus when that executive director has the power to vote the NED off the board.

🔍 EXAMPLE

The following newspaper report provides damning evidence of what has happened in banking boardrooms.

'Despite the losses, Lloyds Banking Group has drawn up plans to pay about £120m in bonuses, the payouts distributed among thousands of workers in Lloyds retail and commercial banking businesses, who received about £150m in bonus payments last year. They are likely to inflame the growing row over City bonuses which was stoked last week by the disclosure that Royal Bank of Scotland, almost 70% owned by the taxpayer, was looking to pay staff as much as £1bn in bonuses this year. Last year, Sir Fred Goodwin, chairman of Royal Bank of Scotland, took home £1.4m, despite the Government's part-nationalisation of RBS, a move that resulted, days later, in Sir Fred's resignation.'

(Source: Weekly Telegraph, Bank chiefs say sorry to MPs, 26 February–4 March 2009)

QUICK RECAP

- *Information provided in business accounts can be analysed into different sections that are easier to assimilate.*
- *P&L statements are presented in a traditional format, though businesses might have different sections according to groupings of major costs.*
- *All businesses invariably show a section that contains direct costs or cost of sales.*
- *Published accounts often include 'notes' that give more detailed information than the totals shown in the actual statement.*
- *Balance sheets are also presented in a traditional format that enables information to be analysed easily.*
- *Checking the values in account statements between two years can tell you about important movements in the business.*
- *Comparing the information from a competitor's accounts with that for your own business can indicate issues that you need to address.*
- *Apply care when looking at data shown in graphical form since it is often more easy to hide questionable performance in eye-catching graphics.*
- *The information contained in the Annual Report and Accounts for a major corporation provides a great deal of information about the business.*

CHAPTER 8

Keeping a check on trends

In the previous chapter we suggested how you can compile your own accounts but that you might want to compare performance over several years to determine whether financial management has become more, or less, efficient over a longer period. You can do this, either in your own organisation or between different businesses, using a process that involves calculating **management ratios**. This chapter explains how to calculate management ratios.

WHAT ARE MANAGEMENT RATIOS?

Because we want to compare values from different periods of time, we have to convert information to common mathematical measures. Most ratios convert values to percentages though other measurements are also used.

Owners and managers want to know that their businesses are operating as efficiently as possible and want to be assured that business performance is in line with the predictions made in the budget. Business efficiency is demonstrated by a positive relationship between income, costs and profit and is viable when it has:

- Achieved the required level of sales income for products sold.
- Controlled its costs while producing the required level of sales income.
- Produced an acceptable level of profit.

Management ratios represent the relationship between these factors and enable managers to monitor business performance by checking movements in those relationships over time. Traditionally, management ratios are grouped into categories, including:

- Cost and profitability ratios.
- Working capital ratios.
- Productivity ratios.

Cost and profitability ratios

Cost and profitability ratios enable you to check the movements and relationships between income, costs and profit. You can use the changes in results to compare the performances between months or years. If you can get financial information about your competitors, you can also use these ratios to check the performance of your business against your competitors' performance.

You calculate cost and profitability ratios using the following formulae:

$$\frac{\text{Cost of sales}}{\text{Total sales income}} \times 100 = \text{Production efficiency}$$

$$\frac{\text{Overheads}}{\text{Total sales income}} \times 100 = \text{Management efficiency}$$

$$\frac{\text{Total costs}}{\text{Total sales income}} \times 100 = \text{Business efficiency}$$

$$\frac{\text{Net profit before tax}}{\text{Total sales income}} \times 100 = \text{Profit efficiency}$$

In order to demonstrate how ratios are calculated, we will use the information for 2007 from the StoneGlass accounts. You can find a complete table of StoneGlass's accounts in Appendix A at the end of this book.

Q CASE STUDY

To determine how the business had changed during the last few years, the Stone family decided to calculate ratios for the years 2007 to 2009 and to compare the results with the budget for 2010. They started by calculating cost and profitability ratios for 2007 as follows:

$$\frac{\text{Cost of sales}}{\text{Total sales income}} \times 100 = \frac{£1,672,300}{£2,230,000} \times 100 = 74.95\%$$

$$\frac{\text{Overheads}}{\text{Total sales income}} \times 100 = \frac{£174,300}{£2,230,000} \times 100 = 7.82\%$$

$$\frac{\text{Total costs}}{\text{Total sales income}} \times 100 = \frac{£1,846,600}{£2,230,000} \times 100 = 82.76\%$$

$$\frac{\text{Net profit before tax}}{\text{Total sales income}} \times 100 = \frac{£384,400}{£2,230,000} \times 100 = 17.24\%$$

The Stones decided to create a table of ratios to which they could add more values, and compare results, as they were calculated:

	2007	2008	2009	2010 Budget
Production efficiency	74.95			
Management efficiency	7.82			
Business efficiency	82.76			
Profit efficiency	17.24			

ACTION POINT

To ensure that you understand how to calculate and use ratios, complete the calculation of the ratios for the other years in the table. When you have completed the table, think about what the results tell you about the efficiency of StoneGlass. What actions would you take in these circumstances? You can check your conclusions with ours when we go through all the ratios and analyse the performance of StoneGlass later in this chapter.

Notice that we have calculated profit achieved against sales income to tell us how efficient the business is at producing profits. However, a business owner also wants to know the level of return achieved on his or her investment in the business, and perhaps how the profit achieved compares with other forms of investment. We can calculate this value using a ratio called **return on capital employed (RoCE)**, which measures the return that a business generates on the money invested in the business and is calculated using the following formula:

$$\frac{\text{Net profit before tax} \times 100}{\text{Owner(s) equity}} = \text{Return on capital employed (RoCE)}$$

🔍 CASE STUDY

The RoCE calculation for 2007 was calculated as follows:

$$\frac{\text{Net profit before tax} \times 100}{\text{Owner(s) equity}} = \frac{£384,400 \times 100}{£324.400} = 118.50\%$$

In 2007 the business achieved an excellent return on the money invested in the business. This return could be checked against other investment opportunities, such as bank interest, though the business had achieved rather more than bank interest would pay:

	2007	2008	2009	2010 Budget
Production efficiency	74.95			
Management efficiency	7.82			
Business efficiency	82.76			
Profit efficiency	17.24			
Return on capital employed	118.50			

When you calculate RoCE, you need to think seriously about how you define the equity in your business. For example, equity can be defined as 'the finance used to fund the business'; in this case you might decide that a long-term loan is capital invested and employed in the business and should be treated, for the purpose of the ratio, as part of equity. You have to decide what makes up the total investment in your business, but once you have made your decision you *must* stick to that definition for all future calculations to be able to compare like with like in future years.

One of the issues that you need to consider about a long-term loan is how vulnerable that loan will make your business. Over the past few years, it has become a 'norm' for businesses to borrow extensively in order to expand, assuming that increasing profits will more than cover loan and interest repayments and that the investment will increase owners' equity in the long-term. Unfortunately, this does not always happen:

🔍 EXAMPLE

During 2008-2009 a number of 'high street' retail businesses found that their sales were drastically reduced as a result of the credit crunch and employee redundancies, both of which reduced the ability of consumers to spend money. Many retail chains had borrowed heavily to open more shops and expand and many were unable to continue to service their loans. Well known names such as Woolworths and Barratts went into receivership.

In order to check the validity of long-term loans, you can calculate a **capital gearing ratio**, which measures the relationship between owner's equity and the value of long-term loans using the following formula:

$$\frac{\text{Long-term liabilities}}{\text{Owners' equity}} \times 100 = \text{Capital gearing ratio \%}$$

Q CASE STUDY

Because StoneGlass had no long-term borrowing in 2007, the business was not able to calculate this ratio for that year. However, we deal with gearing as a separate issue later in this book.

Lenders usually insist that a loan should be matched in value by the amount of capital invested in a business, and look favourably on a business when owners' equity exceeds the amount of long-term loans. For this reason, it is generally considered that the capital gearing ratio should not exceed 100% of equity in any year, though a lender will take into account the gearing sensitivity of the business, which depends on whether the business *has* to borrow large amounts of money in order to operate.

Some businesses are very 'gearing sensitive'; a business that operates hotels must invest heavily in hotel premises, resulting in it being highly geared. Similarly, an airline's fixed assets (aircraft and maintenance buildings) are very costly, which again results in high gearing ratios in this industry.

A business that operates with a very low gearing ratio can be perceived as being very narrow because low borrowing can suggest that the owner(s) are risk averse and are failing to grasp opportunities for expansion, because they are reluctant to take on more debt to grow the business. Business expansion is really a matter of personal choice, depending on the long-term objectives of the owner(s), and you should not pay too much attention to any accusation of being too risk-conscious. As we have illustrated with the retail shops example above, borrowing too much can be fatal to your business.

TOP TIPS

Businesses that are heavily influenced by American management refer to capital gearing as capital leverage.

✍ ACTION POINT

Complete the calculation of the RoCE for the other years in the table and the capital gearing ratio for 2010. When you have completed the table, think about what the results tell you about the return that the StoneGlass family are achieving on their investment. What actions would you take in these circumstances?

While the ratios we have calculated so far look at the operational performance of the business, we also need to identify how well the business uses money invested and profits generated. For this we calculate **working capital ratios**.

WORKING CAPITAL RATIOS

Working capital ratios look at the relationship between different factors that make up the working capital in the business.

Working capital ratios are measured as mathematical relationships, or as a number of days rather than as percentages.

Current ratio

We can start with the **current ratio**, which looks at the relationship between current assets and current, or short-term, liabilities. When we calculate the current ratio, we are checking that the value of current assets in the business, at any point, is sufficient to meet current liabilities. The formula for the current ratio is:

$$\frac{\text{Current assets}}{\text{Current liabilities}} = \text{Current ratio (margin of current liability cover)}$$

The objective of a business is to manage working capital so that current assets are equal to, or more than, current liabilities, though many businesses aim for a proportion of 2:1, or £2 of assets for every £1 of liabilities. A ratio of 2:1 means that the business is unlikely to come under financial pressure.

In some ways, this is a cash flow ratio because it measures the way that cash is being used on a day-to-day basis.

✍️ ACTION POINT

Look at the values that are used in the calculation of the current ratio. Bearing in mind the assumption that the business has enough asset value to pay its debts, is there anything that worries you about how this ratio is made up?

The current ratio assumes that the business can convert current assets into cash in order to pay liabilities but, in most businesses, it is extremely difficult to sell stock materials quickly or at the value paid for them. This means that, if the total of the working capital assets contains a large amount of stock, the business might not be able to generate enough short-term cash to meet its short-term liabilities. In order to be confident that your business can pay its short-term accounts without selling stock, you can calculate the current ratio but exclude the value of any stock; this ratio is then known as the **acid test** or **quick ratio**.

Acid test or quick ratio

The acid test or quick ratio excludes assets that cannot be converted into cash quickly. In most businesses, this means that the ratio does not include the benefit of inventory and is calculated using the following formula:

$$\frac{\text{Short-term cash assets (Current assets – Inventory)}}{\text{Current liabilities}} = \text{Liabilities cover}$$

🔍 CASE STUDY

The current ratio and acid test were calculated for the business for 2007 as follows:

$$\frac{\text{Current assets}}{\text{Current liabilities}} = \frac{£539,400}{£520,000} = 1.04$$

$$\frac{\text{Current assets – Inventory}}{\text{Current liabilities}} = \frac{£539,400 – £211,600}{£520,000} = \frac{£327,800}{£520\ 000} = 0.63$$

Since the acid test showed that 'cash assets' did not cover liabilities, the Stone family began to understand why the business seemed to be continually under pressure for payment of supplier accounts. They added these values to the ratio table:

	2007	2008	2009	2010 Budget
Production efficiency	74.95			
Management efficiency	7.82			
Business efficiency	82.76			
Profit efficiency	17.24			
Return on capital employed	118.50			
Current ratio	1.04			
Acid test	0.63			

ACTION POINT

Complete the calculations for the current ratio and acid test for the other years in the table and think about what the results tell you about how the Stone family are managing working capital. What actions would you take in these circumstances?

While the acid test provides a good reference to the ability of a business to pay its short-term liabilities, we have to recognise that not all customers pay their accounts on time. Therefore, we need to check how efficiently the business collects payments due in from customers, or debtors. To do this we calculate the **debtor management ratio**.

Debtor management ratio

We can measure the efficiency of debt collection by looking at the relationship between outstanding debtors and turnover, and by identifying how many days, on average, it takes the business to collect payments of accounts due from customers. The formula for the debtor management ratio is as follows:

$$\frac{\text{Debtors} \times 365}{\text{Turnover}} = \text{Debtor collection days}$$

This calculation gives us the number of days, on average through the year, it has taken a business to collect due accounts from its customers. The result for an efficient business should be close to the number of days' credit that the business allows to its customers.

The 'norm' in relation to the debtor management ratio depends on the type of business that you operate. A cash business or retail shop will show a very low number of collection days because customers pay immediately and the only unpaid accounts are those relating to the few days required to clear credit card or cheque payments. A building business may be paid in stages so that the normal credit arrangements can be for 60 days or even 90 days.

If you aim to manage your debtor accounts efficiently, it is also fair to assume that you should manage your creditor accounts equally efficiently. You can check this by calculating the **creditor management ratio**.

Creditor management ratio

The calculation to measure how well a business pays its creditor accounts is similar to the ratio above, except that the formula changes to reflect creditor values as follows:

$$\frac{\text{Creditors} \times 365}{\text{Total costs}} = \text{Creditor payment days}$$

Q CASE STUDY

The Stone family were shaken by the information revealed by the current ratio and acid test and need to check on the cash flowing through the business. Therefore they calculated how well the business received and paid money during 2007 as follows:

$$\frac{\text{Debtors} \times 365}{\text{Turnover}} = \frac{£327,800 \times 365}{£2,230,000} = 53.65 \text{ days}$$

$$\frac{\text{Creditors} \times 365}{\text{Total costs}} = \frac{£353,000 \times 365}{£1,845,900} = 69.81 \text{ days}$$

They realised that they were not collecting overdue accounts in accordance with 30-day credit terms, and that they were far worse in paying their 30-day accounts, taking almost 70 days on average. They added the values to the table and vowed to look at how their efficiency had developed over the years:

	2007	2008	2009	2010 Budget
Production efficiency (%)	74.95			
Management efficiency (%)	7.82			
Business efficiency (%)	82.76			
Profit efficiency (%)	17.24			
Return on capital employed (%)	118.50			
Current ratio	1.04			
Acid test	0.63			
Debtor collection days	53.65			
Creditor payment days	69.81			

It is not unusual to find that debtor and creditor management ratios exceed the normal credit arrangements, but a danger signal shows when a business appears to be very efficient in collecting money from customers but is long overdue on paying its suppliers. This usually indicates a business under financial pressure due to a cash shortage, possibly arising from failing to make adequate profits or using cash to buy unproductive capital assets such as executive cars.

However, cash can also be tied up if the business carries excessive inventory. We can check the validity of stock control by calculating the **inventory management ratio**.

Inventory management ratio

When you buy in materials for stock, or take a long time to convert stock materials into goods for sale, you are tying up cash that you cannot use for other things.

🔍 EXAMPLE

A clothes retailer might buy £10,000 of shirts for which he or she has to pay in 30 days. If the shop does not sell those shirts before the debt has to be paid, it has cash tied up in unsold stocks and perhaps cannot afford to buy other clothes that it needs for the season. Similarly, if StoneGlass buys glass that it cannot convert into saleable goods in a reasonable time, it will have tied up cash that will not come back into the business until the business's products are eventually sold and paid for.

It is extremely important to manage the level of inventory in your business to ensure that you have enough materials to cover your *optimum* level of operation, which means that there should be:
- Enough stock to meet customer demands
- The level that enables materials to be used, if possible, before the suppliers' accounts become due for payment

We can calculate how many days it takes the business to use inventory using the following formula:

$$\frac{\text{Inventory} \times 365}{\text{Direct costs}} = \text{Inventory turnover days}$$

✍️ ACTION POINT

Complete the calculations to check on the efficiency of management of debtors, creditors and inventory for the other years in the table and think about what the results tell you about how the Stone family are managing the working capital of the business. What actions would you take in these circumstances?

Q CASE STUDY

StoneGlass completed its calculation of working capital ratios by calculating its inventory management days for 2007:

$$\frac{\text{Inventory} \times 365}{\text{Direct costs}} = \frac{£211,600 \times 365}{£1,671,300} = 63.41 \text{ days}$$

Adding this ratio to the table, the StoneGlass family realised that it was taking more than two months to convert materials into saleable goods.

	2007	2008	2009	2010 Budget
Production efficiency (%)	74.95			
Management efficiency (%)	7.82			
Business efficiency (%)	82.76			
Profit efficiency (%)	17.24			
Return on capital employed (%)	118.50			
Current ratio	1.04			
Acid test	0.63			
Debtor collection days	53.65			
Creditor payment days	69.81			
Inventory turnover days	63.41			

TOP TIPS

Notice how we have used different factors to establish relationships that are dependent on each other. For example, debtors are related to total income, creditors to total costs and inventory to direct costs.

In a small business, it is usually easy to manage inventory to its most efficient level though it can be a challenge for larger and more complex businesses.

For example, managing materials on a busy construction site can be extremely difficult, not only because of the number of items used but also because of the variety of materials used, such as quantities of sand, cement, bricks, electrical fittings, kitchen and bathroom furniture. Also, imagine how the inventory management ratio would apply to a business that buys in a large number of different parts in order to assemble and manufacture products, such as computers or electricity generators. As a business becomes larger and more complex, inventory management usually becomes more difficult yet more important since the cost to the business of poor management can be very high.

Poor management of working capital factors affects the productivity of a business because of the dangers related to:

- Lack of available materials when required.
- Losses resulting from over-ordered stocks that have become obsolete or damaged.
- Suppliers refusing to deliver more materials because accounts have not been paid.
- Increasing costs resulting from the need to negotiate overdrafts and pay interest and other finance charges.

Since financial management has a direct effect on the productivity of a business, we need to use management ratios called **productivity ratios** to monitor that productivity.

PRODUCTIVITY RATIOS

Productivity ratios measure the productivity of the resources available to the business and the way in which they create income and profit. The resources that contribute to productivity are:

- Fixed or capital assets such as the premises, machinery, equipment, vehicles and fittings used by the business to produce products.
- Personnel assets or the people employed in the business who are often referred to as human resources.

We measure and monitor asset productivity by looking at the relationship between the cost of resources and the levels of turnover and profitability produced by those resources, resulting in the comparisons or ratios that we explain below.

If you operate a small business, you can find that the results of productivity ratios relating to employees do not provide any significant information. This is due to the fact that there is often little change in employees' contribution to the business when there are only one or two employees involved. Therefore, productivity measures are more meaningful to businesses that employ a large range of capital assets and a number of employees in the production processes.

Fixed asset productivity ratios

Fixed asset productivity ratios tell us how efficiently the fixed assets are used to produce turnover and operating, or gross, profit. Therefore, asset productivity ratios are calculated using the following formulae:

$$\frac{\text{Total turnover}}{\text{Total fixed assets}} = \text{Fixed assets productivity (£)}$$

$$\frac{\text{Gross profit}}{\text{Total fixed assets}} = \text{Fixed assets profit generation (£)}$$

Q CASE STUDY

*StoneGlass calculated its fixed asset productivity ratios for
2007 using the above formulae:*

$$\frac{\text{Total turnover}}{\text{Total fixed assets}} = \frac{£2,230,000}{£305,000} = £7.31$$

$$\frac{\text{Gross profit}}{\text{Total fixed assets}} = \frac{£558,700}{£305,000} = £1.83$$

*StoneGlass has identified that, in 2007, every £1 of fixed
assets produced £7.31 in turnover and £1.83 in gross profit.*

Employee productivity ratios

In a similar way to fixed assets, employee productivity is calculated
using the following formulae:

$$\frac{\text{Total turnover}}{\text{Number of employees}} = \text{Employee turnover productivity (£)}$$

$$\frac{\text{Net profit before tax}}{\text{Number of employees}} = \text{Employee profit generation (£)}$$

Q CASE STUDY

StoneGlass calculated its fixed asset productivity ratios for 2007 using the above formulae:

$$\frac{\text{Total turnover}}{\text{Number of employees}} = \frac{£2,230,000}{12} = £185,833$$

$$\frac{\text{Net profit before tax}}{\text{Number of employees}} = \frac{£384,400}{12} = £32,033$$

StoneGlass had identified that, in 2007, each employee had generated £185,833 in turnover and £32,033 in profits before tax. They added this information to the ratios table they had started:

	2007	2008	2009	2010 Budget
Production efficiency (%)	74.95			
Management efficiency (%)	7.82			
Business efficiency (%)	82.76			
Profit efficiency (%)	17.24			
Return on capital employed (%)	118.50			
Current ratio	1.04			
Acid test	0.63			
Debtor collection days	53.65			
Creditor payment days	69.81			
Inventory turnover days	63.41			
Fixed asset productivity (£)	7.31			
Fixed asset profit generation (£)	1.83			
Employee productivity (£)	185,833			
Employee profit generation (£)	32,033			

We calculated fixed asset productivity using gross profit, but employee productivity using net profit because capital assets are used mostly in the production process to produce products and therefore mainly influence the gross, or operating, profit of the business. People are employed throughout the entire business and therefore influence net profit.

In larger organisations, capital assets and employees can be categorised into the areas in which they are used, in which case it is possible to calculate productivity ratios separately for the production and administrative functions.

ACTION POINT

StoneGlass employed 15 people in 2008, 16 people in 2009 and have budgeted for 24 employees in 2010. Now complete the calculations opposite to check on the productivity of the resources used in StoneGlass for the years 2008 through 2010. When you have completed the table, think about what the results tell you about the productivity of StoneGlass resources. What actions would you want to take in these circumstances?

There is one more productivity ratio that we can use to check the relationship of payroll with turnover and net profit, which is called the **payroll productivity ratio**.

Payroll productivity ratio

The payroll productivity ratio identifies when the money paid out in wages and salaries is becoming less efficient in terms of income and profit generated. For example, a business can become more inefficient when it employs unnecessary managers instead of more necessary production staff. Payroll productivity ratio is calculated using the following formulae:

$$\frac{\text{Total turnover}}{\text{Total payroll}} = \text{Payroll productivity (£)}$$

$$\frac{\text{Net profit before tax}}{\text{Total payroll}} = \text{Payroll profit generation (£)}$$

Q CASE STUDY

StoneGlass calculated its fixed asset productivity ratios for 2007 using the above formulae:

$$\frac{\text{Total turnover}}{\text{Total payroll}} = \frac{£2,230,000}{£367,200 + £120,000 + £32,000} = £4.30$$

$$\frac{\text{Net profit before tax}}{\text{Total payroll}} = \frac{£384,400}{£367,200 + £120,000 + £32,000} = £0.74$$

This shows that, in 2007, every £1 that the business paid in wages and salaries produced £4.30 in sales income and £0.74 in net profit before tax and StoneGlass added this information to complete the ratio table as follows:

	2007	2008	2009	2010 Budget
Production efficiency (%)	74.95			
Management efficiency (%)	7.82			
Business efficiency (%)	82.76			
Profit efficiency (%)	17.24			
Return on capital employed (%)	118.50			
Current ratio	1.04			
Acid test	0.63			
Debtor collection days	53.65			
Creditor payment days	69.81			
Inventory turnover days	63.41			
Fixed asset productivity (£)	7.31			
Fixed asset profit generation (£)	1.83			

Employee productivity (£)	185,833			
Employee profit generation (£)	32,033			
Payroll productivity (3)	4.30			
Payroll profit generation (£)	0.74			

ACTION POINT

Complete the calculations for the above table by calculating the payroll productivity ratios for the years 2008 through 2010. When you have completed the table, think about what the results tell you about the productivity of StoneGlass's resources. What actions would you want to take in these circumstances?

USING FINANCIAL DATA TO IMPROVE MANAGEMENT PERFORMANCE

When you calculate management ratios over several years, you have a body of data that tells you a great deal about the business and provides sound information on which you can make decisions for improvement. As you have seen during this chapter, we calculated a number of different ratios that gave us information about the performance of StoneGlass for the 2007 trading year. At each stage in the development of ratios, we asked you to practise your prowess at calculating and interpreting the information you

built up and you should by now have the following full table for
StoneGlass:

	2007	2008	2009	2010 Budget
Production efficiency (%)	74.95	77.42	90.61	78.41
Management efficiency (%)	7.82	8.36	9.30	12.00
Business efficiency (%)	82.76	85.78	99.91	90.41
Profit efficiency (%)	17.24	14.23	0.09	9.59
Return on capital employed (%)	118.50	72.56	0.53	51.94
Current ratio	1.04	1.45	1.37	2.93
Acid test	0.63	0.82	0.74	2.03
Gearing	0	0	0	125.91
Debtor collection days	53.65	63.30	60.03	34.46
Creditor payment days	69.81	58.12	55.49	46.95
Inventory turnover days	63.41	88.91	81.70	70.63
Fixed asset productivity (£)	7.31	9.90	12.65	5.17
Fixed asset profit generation (£)	1.83	2.23	1.19	1.12
Employee productivity (£)	185,833	191,333	217,500	179,167
Employee profit generation (£)	32,033	27,220	188	17,188
Payroll productivity (3)	4.30	3.82	3.29	3.77
Payroll profit generation (£)	0.74	0.54	0	0.36

ACTION POINT:

Check your calculations against the above table to make sure that you agree. If you have any differences, recheck your calculation so that you are confident that you understand how each ratio is calculated.

When you calculate ratios, it is a good idea to calculate them to two decimal places, because that enables you to identify small changes that can signify the development of a trend that could become significant over time. In the above table, we did not follow that advice for employee ratios because two decimal places would be insignificant in the level of these values.

We are now in a position to assess the performance of the business between 2007 and 2009, plus the performance that the business has budgeted for during 2010. We need to remember that the owners set the 2010 budget in the face of a very low profit in 2009 and with some determination to improve the performance of the business. To help their strategy, they have borrowed £1m and invested a good proportion of that in new machinery.

In order to look objectively at the performance of the business over the years, we will look at the above ratios in the groups in which we explained them previously, though we may need to refer to other ratios from time to time.

Assessing the performance of cost and profitability ratios

Since these ratios assess the relationship between costs, profits and turnover, we want to see that, over several years:

- Direct costs as a proportion of turnover, or the measure of production efficiency, are falling.
- Overheads as a proportion of turnover, or the measure of management efficiency, are falling.
- Total costs as a proportion of turnover, or the measure of business efficiency, are falling.

- The profit efficiency of the business is rising.
- The return on investment generated by the business is higher than other investment options and is rising with time.

🔍 CASE STUDY

The owners of the business studied the cost and profitability ratios that they had prepared for the years from 2007 to 2010, which they extracted as follows:

	2007	2008	2009	2010 Budget
Production efficiency (%)	74.95	77.42	90.61	78.41
Management efficiency (%)	7.82	8.36	9.30	12.00
Business efficiency (%)	82.76	85.78	99.91	90.41
Profit efficiency (%)	17.24	14.23	0.09	9.59
Return on capital employed (%)	118.50	72.56	0.53	51.94

After much deliberation and discussion, they realised that:

- *They had failed to manage direct costs as a proportion of turnover, which were less than 75% in 2007 but had been allowed to rise to the disastrous level of 91% in 2009.*
- *They had failed to register the clear warning in 2009, and had budgeted a direct cost level of over 78% for 2010.*
- *They had failed to manage overheads as a proportion of turnover, which had risen from less than 8% in 2007 to 12% in 2010.*
- *As a result of the lack of strict management, profits had fallen from over 17% in 2007 to a budgeted 9.69% in 2010 and the return on investment had fallen from more than 118% to a budgeted 52%.*
- *The business was clearly capable of working on a direct cost proportion of less than 75% and an overhead proportion of less than 8%, which meant that a net profit of 17% should*

have been easily achievable even without the more efficient machinery in which they had invested.

The owners resolved to seek out the source of the problems and implement the changes necessary to bring net profits before tax closer to 20% for 2010. They then turned their attention to the working capital ratios.

ACTION POINT

Were your observations different from those of the Stone family? (You could have spotted something they missed). What would you do to address the issues identified?

Assessing the performance of working capital ratios

Working capital ratios assess the way in which the cash flowing through the business has been managed and look for the following benchmarks:

- The ability of the business to *easily* meet its liabilities, which is measured by the acid test.
- Recognition that the business collects money from customers within the normal credit terms allowed, which is measured by debtor management days.
- Recognition that the business pays its suppliers on time, which is measured by the creditor management days.
- The efficiency of the business in managing its stocks and work-in-progress efficiently within the scope of production capabilities and marketplace conditions, which is measured by inventory turnover days.

Q CASE STUDY

The owners of the business studied the working capital ratios that they had prepared for the years from 2007 to 2010, which they extracted as follows:

	2007	2008	2009	2010 Budget
Current ratio	1.04	1.45	1.37	2.93
Acid test	0.63	0.82	0.74	2.03
Debtor collection days	53.65	63.30	60.03	34.46
Creditor payment days	69.81	58.12	55.49	46.95
Inventory turnover days	63.41	88.91	81.70	70.63

Upon investigation, they noted that:

- *While the acid test values for 2007 to 2009 did not supply the cover recommended, they had budgeted for a significant improvement in 2010.*
- *The improvement recorded for 2010 was the result of the loan negotiated, which provided working cash that eliminated the bank overdraft.*
- *They had failed to collect customer payments within the normal 30-days credit terms agreed, though they had budgeted for a significant improvement in 2010.*
- *Possibly as a result of failing to get customers to pay on time, they had failed to pay suppliers on time, though again they had budgeted for an improvement in 2010.*
- *With the fear that suppliers might refuse to deliver further materials until they were paid, the business had 'stock-piled' more materials than it needed for normal operations, with the result that they had enough materials for over two months' production even though finished goods were sold to customers within 14 days.*

Thinking about the issues they had identified, they concluded that they would have to employ someone to chase payments from customers and to more efficiently control payments to suppliers, which would enable them to reduce the quantity of 'safety' stocks held. However, they then became concerned that employing another individual would make their overhead management even worse, so they decided that they would have to think about it some more and move on to look at productivity ratios.

ACTION POINT

Were your observations different from those of the Stone family? (You could have spotted something they missed). What would you do to address the issues identified?

Assessing the performance of productivity ratios

Productivity ratios assess the performance of the resources used in the business and look for the following performance measurements:

- Fixed assets producing an increasing level of productivity, by delivering more products, as the value declines because of depreciation.
- Fixed assets providing an increasing level of profit as the value decreases because of depreciation.
- Employees producing an increasing level of productivity, in terms of products produced, as the sale prices of products increases.
- Employees producing an increasing level of profits as they become more experienced and therefore more productive.
- The money paid out in wages and salaries resulting in increasing profits to confirm that the employees appointed are at least covering the costs of their employment.

🔍 CASE STUDY

The owners of the business studied the productivity ratios that they had prepared for the years from 2007 to 2010, which they extracted as follows:

	2007	2008	2009	2010 Budget
Fixed asset productivity (£)	7.31	9.90	12.65	5.17
Fixed asset profit generation (£)	1.83	2.23	1.19	1.12
Employee productivity (£)	185,833	191,333	217,500	179,167
Employee profit generation (£)	32,033	27,220	188	17,188
Payroll productivity (£)	4.30	3.82	3.29	3.77
Payroll profit generation (£)	0.74	0.54	0	0.36

After investigation, they reached the following conclusions:

- *They were pleased that fixed asset productivity was positive in terms of goods produced until the installation of the new machines in 2010.*
- *While the productivity of fixed assets was positive for the years 2007 to 2009, the generation of profits had fallen off to a low of £1.19 for every £1 of assets.*
- *Employee productivity improved well over the 2007 to 2009 years though, surprisingly, it was projected to fall back in 2010.*
- *The ability of employees to produce profits was disappointing, in view of their good productivity record.*
- *The ability of the payroll to generate profits had also fallen, which the owners found confusing in view of the sound productivity figures.*

With the mass of information available, the owners found themselves going round in circles as they argued about the reasons for their apparent inefficiencies. How could they possibly be showing adverse ratios in 2010 when they had worked so hard to introduce new machines and improve the profitability that they had lost in 2009? After hours of discussion, they decided that they had to go away and individually consider what should be done before meeting again to agree a plan for improvement.

ACTION POINT

Were your observations different from those of the Stone family? (You could have spotted something they missed). What would you do to address the issues identified?

PLANNING FOR IMPROVEMENTS

When faced with a mass of data such as that produced for StoneGlass, you have to apply your overall knowledge of the business, but ask pertinent questions that might include the following:

- Are my product prices set at the correct level for the marketplace?
- If I apply a zero-based approach to the production unit (or retail unit) for my business unit, what savings can I make?
- Are our direct production employees fully employed by the current level of sales or do I have production employees who are 'coasting'?
- Are our administration employees fully employed by the current level of operation or do I have employees who are 'coasting'?
- How efficient are our administrative systems? Do our administrative systems need to be upgraded? Do we have too many staff?

- How do our salaries compare with other local businesses? Are our salaries too high?
- Who is responsible for chasing customer accounts and paying customer accounts? Do we have the right person in the job(s)? Have they been trained to do the jobs efficiently and well?
- Why are we carrying so much stock? Are our buyers receiving perks from suppliers to order more materials than we need?
- Do we have the right machines for the work we need?
- Have employees been properly trained to use machines and get the best performance from those machines?

As you can see, we are asking questions that are total business related rather than focused on one or more ratios, though the answers will impact on one or more ratios and we can use the ratios to help us find the answers. You might feel that the zero-based question is inappropriate at this point since it should have been applied at the point of creating the budget. If you have a business that is successful in its marketplace, there are often ways to achieve an extra saving through the zero-based approach.

🔍 EXAMPLE

Waitrose wrote to 1,000 of its suppliers to ask them to reduce their prices by 2pc as the John Lewis Partnership-owned supermarket looked to cut costs in the face of the consumer downturn. Managing director, Mark Price, said that the requests had gone to suppliers of branded foods and farmers in the UK following a fall in commodity prices, meaning that suppliers' raw materials costs were cheaper. He also said that suppliers were set to profit from Waitrose's growth, so should share the benefits. In total, Waitrose had around 2,500 suppliers at the time.

(Source: James Hall , Weekly Telegraph, 19-25 March 2009)

🔍 CASE STUDY

The Stone family discussed the ideas that they had generated and met to consolidate the reasons that performance had fallen and to create a plan for improvements. They used the above list of questions as a basis for their discussion and agreed the following issues were the most relevant to their business:

- *When they considered the purchase of the new machines, they had been anxious about selling the additional production, even though their marketplace survey indicated that their products were popular and demand was high. They now realised that they had mistakenly decided to reduce prices to make their products more competitive when they did not need to do so, and that decision meant that cost and profitability ratios had become 'out of sync':*
- **They decided that since they had not yet announced the new prices for 2010, they would revert back to the old prices, which would increase turnover by 10%.**
- *When they created the flexed budget for 2010 they had applied a zero-based approach to the previous year's costs, but they realised that they had not tried to negotiate with major suppliers for discounts to reflect the additional production planned:*
- **A call to the materials suppliers resulted in an agreed saving of 5% provided that accounts were paid in accordance with credit terms.**
- *Looking at the planned employee numbers for 2010, the increase of eight employees that they had estimated would be required included five production employees and three administrative staff:*
- **On examination, they realised that the additional production would come from the new machines and they did not need additional production employees.**
- *With hindsight, they realised that they could personally take responsibility for administrative tasks such as chasing debtors and ensuring credit accounts were paid on time and that the increased turnover would result in very little additional administrative work:*
- **They found that, provided the family members became more involved with administration, they would not**

have to replace a retiring staff member and they would not need the additional staff planned.

- *They needed to provide a more efficient accounting system that would provide monthly management information, including debtor and creditor lists:*
- **To this end they decided to update their software, which they could do within the present budget.**
- *One of the family members had reviewed the rates of wages and salaries paid against other local businesses and found that StoneGlass's rates were a little higher than the prevailing rates in the area:*
- **In view of all the changes they were making and their desire to retain good trained employees, they decided to keep remuneration at the present level but review it at the end of each year. Again in the light of the present situation, the family decided that they should not give themselves a salary increase for 2010 but should review that once they could see that the changes were working.**
- *With the new efficiency measures in mind, they decided to allocate vital responsibilities:*
- **They agreed which family member would be responsible for each of the tasks – chasing debtor accounts, paying creditors, preparing month-end management accounts and managing the inventory.**
- *Now with one of the family responsible for managing the inventory, and with the new agreement with suppliers in mind:*
- **They agreed that it should be possible to quickly reduce current levels and maintain stocks to a level of 30 days production.**
- *Having purchased new machines, they were certain that the ones they had bought were correct for the job required. However, they were still using some older equipment:*
- **As a result of this they decided to review all equipment during the year with a view to replacing with more efficient equipment as soon as possible.**
- **Since they intended to seek maximum efficiency in future, they decided to review all systems during the year and to implement training courses for all employees in 2011 in order to improve the skills available to the business.**

Having made these decisions, they reviewed the budget for 2010 and produced the following changes from the 2010 budget set:

P&L Budget	2010	2010
	Set	Revised
Turnover	4,300,000	4,730,000
Direct costs:		
Materials	2,310,000	2,194,500
Wages	850,000	807,500
Employee costs	57,000	54,150
Maintenance	8,000	8,000
Depreciation	73,500	73,500
Electricity	18,000	18,000
Water	2,000	2,000
Consumables	4,000	4,000
Packaging costs	12,000	12,000
Business rates	22,000	22,000
Insurance	15,000	15,000
Total direct costs	3,371,500	3,210,650
Gross profit	928,500	1,519,350
Overheads:		
Owners salaries	200,000	180,000
Admin salaries	90,000	85,500
Employee costs	30,000	28,500
Design costs	80,000	80,000
Marketing	10,000	10,000
Stationery	3,000	3,000
Telephone & post	8,000	8,000
Maintenance	2,000	2,000
Emp consumables	1,000	1,000
Loan interest	80,000	80,000
Audit	7,000	7,000
Bank charges	5,000	5,000
Total overheads	516,000	490,000
Net profit before tax	412,500	1,029,350
Less: Tax	180,000	300,000
Retained profit	232,500	729,350

BS Budget	2010	2010
	Set	Revised
Fixed assets:	831,500	831,500
Premises	200,000	200,000
Machinery	621,500	621,500
Office	10,000	10,000
Current assets:	1,462,700	1,992,050
Inventory	447,000	197,000
Debtors	406,000	400,000
Cash at bank	609,700	1,395,050
Current liabilities:	500,000	300,000
Creditors	500,000	300,000
Bank overdraft	0	0
Long-term liabilities:	1,000,000	1,000,000
Loan	1,000,000	1,000,000
Net assets	794,200	1,523,550
Equity:	794,200	1,523,550
Owners investment	50,000	50,000
Retained profits	744,200	1,473,550

Having revised the budget for 2010, the family decided that they should also update the ratios table to reflect the new budget, which then appeared as follows:

	2007	2008	2009	2010 Set budget	2010 Revised budget
Production efficiency (%)	74.95	77.42	90.61	78.41	67.88
Management efficiency (%)	7.82	8.36	9.30	12.00	10.36
Business efficiency (%)	82.76	85.78	99.91	90.41	78.24
Profit efficiency (%)	17.24	14.23	0.09	9.59	21.76
Return on capital employed (%)	118.50	72.56	0.53	51.94	67.56
Current ratio	1.04	1.45	1.37	2.93	6.64
Acid test	0.63	0.82	0.74	2.03	5.98
Gearing	0	0	0	125.91	65.64
Debtor collection days	53.65	63.30	60.03	34.46	30.87
Creditor payment days	69.81	58.12	55.49	46.95	29.59
Inventory turnover days	63.41	88.91	81.70	70.63	32.77
Fixed asset productivity (£)	7.31	9.90	12.65	5.17	5.69
Fixed asset profit generation (£)	1.83	2.23	1.19	1.12	1.83
Employee productivity (£)	185 833	191 333	217 500	179 167	295625
Employee profit generation (£)	32 033.00	27 220	188	17 188	64334
Payroll productivity (£)	4.30	3.82	3.29	3.77	4.41
Payroll profit generation (£)	0.74	0.54	0	0.36	0.96

When they looked at the revised ratios table, the family members were delighted because they could see that, provided that they managed the business efficiently, they would achieve:

- *The highest production efficiency in the history of the business.*
- *The best level of net profit before tax in the history of the business.*
- *A return on capital invested of almost 70%.*
- *Very efficient management of working capital.*
- *A bank balance of more than £1m that would enable them to pay off some of the loan faster while retaining enough cash in the business to continue its smooth operation.*
- *A complete turnaround from the disastrous results of 2009.*
- *A great deal of motivation to make the changes happen.*

In the analyses that we have carried out in this chapter, you might have noticed that we did not talk about the gearing ratio. We should do that now to complete the analysis.

ADDRESSING THE GEARING RATIO

We excluded any consideration of the gearing ratio in the performance of StoneGlass because the business had not required any borrowing for the years to 2009, which gave us no ratios for comparison. However, having set the budget for 2010 and then having carried out the revisions discussed above, we can see the effect that that has had on the gearing ratio as follows:

	2007	2008	2009	2010 Set budget	2010 Revised budget
Gearing	0	0	0	125.91	65.64

When we talked about this ratio earlier, we indicated that a business should normally try to limit borrowing to the level of equity in the business. During the past few years, it has become common practice for businesses of all types, though particularly in the retail sector, to borrow excessively to fund expansion with the result that, if demand for products falls lower incomes cannot fund the interest and repayments scheduled and businesses can fail. This suggests that the traditional measure of gearing – that it should ideally sit somewhere between 50% and 100% of equity – is soundly based.

In the case of the StoneGlass loan, the original budget suggested that the loan would be too high in terms of a gearing ratio of 125%, though the efficiency savings that created the revised budget for 2010 have brought the gearing ratio into the 'ideal' range at 66%. This indicates that gearing is not just about borrowing within your means (in relation to equity) but is about managing the effects of gearing to the most optimal level to produce the profitability that enables the business to meet its loan commitments.

This does raise another issue relating to ratio analysis, which is that while StoneGlass has been able to use the traditional ratios to manage the business, there might be some types of business that need different ratios.

DESIGNING RATIOS TO SUIT YOUR BUSINESS

🔍 EXAMPLE

A business manufacturing clothing had a product range that comprised several different styles, each manufactured in a choice of three or four colours; customers were mainly large multiple stores groups who ordered monthly to top up stock shown on the racks. Garment styles had different cloth contents and took different times to manufacture.

Traditional cost and profitability ratios were calculated monthly but the fluctuations in the values, resulting from the variations in the quantities of different styles ordered, meant that the ratios were valueless in terms of comparison between months. If stores ordered only the cheapest garments, the results were significantly different from a month when more expensive garments were ordered.

As a result, the business designed ratios based on daily production that gave management the level of profit required from that day. In time, the business was able to add an opportunity cost to lower priced products in order to 'balance' the profit to the business irrespective of the prices and balance of the garments ordered.

When you are considering how you can use management ratios in your business, you need to decide:

- If traditional ratios provide the guidance you need to ensure optimum performance of the business.
- At what periods you will calculate ratios.
- What are the significant factors in your business that represent the profit-making focus of the operation? In the above example, that became the number of garments in each range manufactured every day.
- If you need to consider adding an opportunity cost to lower priced products to 'balance' the profit you receive from all products in your range.
- What ratios you should design to manage your business's performance efficiently.

When you have the answers to these questions, you can decide if you need to design specific ratios to give you the best indicators of performance in your particular business unit.

ACTION POINT

What are the most significant factors in your business that you need to monitor? How often do you need to check that your business is operating according to your expectations? Are traditional ratios appropriate for your business or are there other measures that would be more meaningful? Would this be a good point to design special ratios appropriate to your business?

🔍 EXAMPLE

'Taylor Wimpey has more than £1.5bn in debt and is one of a number of house-builders that are struggling with large debts after a round of consolidation in the sector. The firm has been in danger of breaching banking covenants since a failed fund-raising last year. The house-builder has agreed to debt covenants based on cash flow and gearing, as opposed to earnings, which is more in line with its rivals.'

(Source: Nic Fildes , Weekly Telegraph, 9-15 April 2009)

In other words, Taylor Wimpey had discovered that the ratio between debt and earnings was not an adequate measure to protect the business and were moving to ratios that measured debt against cash flow and equity.

When you design your own ratios, it is a good idea to check if they work by carrying out calculations for past performances of the business. If you look back over the past two or more trading periods, the calculations you carry out for the periods you have already experienced will tell you if your ratios are meaningful and provide the information you need to protect your business in the future.

QUICK RECAP

- *The quality of financial management can be assessed using management ratios to assess whether financial management is becoming more or less efficient.*
- *Cost and profitability ratios look at how well costs are being managed against the turnover achieved.*
- *Working capital ratios look at how efficiently the business is managing the cash flowing through it.*
- *Productivity ratios look at the benefits achieved from the resources employed in the business.*
- *A ratios table for several trading periods will quickly show the issues on which you need to concentrate to improve specific areas of your business.*
- *You do not have to use traditional ratios, but can design your own ratios that more accurately reflect your business operation.*
- *If you design your own ratios, check that they work by calculating those ratios for past trading periods that you have experienced.*

CHAPTER 9

Managing external financial influences

When economists look at business operations, they talk about external, marketplace factors that owners and managers should take into account, such as:

- Political influences resulting from Government initiatives and changes in laws and regulations.
- Economic factors relating to global trade and the impact on your business of events in other countries as well as at home, such as the effects of the so called 'credit crunch'.
- Socio-economic factors reflecting the changing attitudes of customers and consumers that arise from changing fashions and attitudes, or perhaps forced on them by other factors.
- Technological innovations that give advantages to those who adopt the new technologies first.

You might find the above factors referred to as PEST or STEP factors, with the acronyms representing the first letters of each item.

Most businesses have very little control over these external factors and, at best, can stay alert to changes and react to the impact at the earliest opportunity. We have introduced you to variance analysis and management ratios to help you to do that. However, you might need to monitor certain issues more closely, such as:

- Ratio of turnover growth.
- Customer purchasing preferences.
- Effects of currency exchange rates.

TURNOVER RATIO

To businesses that sell high volume/low priced products, the levels of turnover achieved, or the level of market share achieved, is of great importance. Another management ratio monitors changes in turnover between trading periods.

Q CASE STUDY

The Stone family decided that they needed to check movements in turnover during the period from 2007 to 2010 and calculated the turnover ratio using the following formula:

Turnover for new year – Turnover for previous year x 100 = Turnover ratio
Turnover for previous year

£2,870,000 (2008) – £2,230,000 (2007) x 100 = 28.70 for 2008
£2,230,000 (2007)

This showed that turnover had increased by 28.70% in 2008. Calculations of following years produced the following:

	2007	2008	2009	2010 Set budget	2010 Revised budget
Turnover ratio (%)	?	28.70	21.25	23.56	35.92

StoneGlass had a 'static' or even declining turnover growth rate for 2009–2010 on the original set budget but could achieve a substantial growth for the revised budget.

However, turnover grows as a result of two factors:
- Price increases that reflect inflation.
- Increasing sales in the volume of products.

For high volume/low price businesses, achieving a price-only increase in turnover can actually mean that the business is standing still or possibly losing market share. To understand what the turnover ratio really represents, you adjust the increase in turnover ratio by the inflation index that you calculated earlier in this book, which adjusts the above information as follows:

	2010 Revised budget
Turnover ratio calculated (%)	35.92
Adjust for 5% inflation by applying 0.95 index	34.12

StoneGlass can now be assured that the budgeted turnover increase for 2010 represents a 2% increase due to inflation plus 34% increase in higher sales volumes, a real expansion of the business.

ACTION POINT

Calculate turnover ratios for your business for the past few years and adjust the ratios for inflation. Did you achieve a real growth increase in sales volumes or was the increase only a reflection of inflation?

CUSTOMER PURCHASING PREFERENCES

In the example of a garment manufacturer used earlier, we suggested that the business might want to apply opportunity costs to low-priced products to protect its profit margins. If you have products with a wide variance in sales prices, you might also have the problem that selling only the low-priced products could result in minimal profitability.

Consumers have become more price conscious in recent years due to competitor advertising focusing on 'special offer' pricing, and are more willing to 'shop around' to secure the best prices for the products they want. This means that there is always the danger that customers might buy only the lower priced products from your business and, as a result, your profit will be minimised. To guard against this possibility, you can apply opportunity costs.

Q EXAMPLE

A small specialist retailer buys in three different ranges of cosmetics:

- *A cheap range to get customers into the shop.*
- *A popular range that represents the base product range of the business.*
- *A gift range to provide special occasion gifts.*

The financial characteristics of the business are as follows:

	Cheap range	Popular range	Gift range
Product quantity	100,000	60,000	10,000
Turnover	280,000	258,000	124,000
Total costs	252,000	206,400	74,400
Profit	28,000	51,600	49,600

The retailer hopes to sell products across the range with a concentration on the 'popular' range that would give an average profit of around £50,000 per annum. However, local supermarkets are offering similar 'popular' and 'gift' range products with the result that the business is attracting more young people who buy only the 'cheap' range of products. With the threat of falling profits, the retailer decides to add an opportunity cost of 10% to the prices of 'cheap' range products so that a focus on sales in that range will not diminish overall profitability. The financial results now appear as follows:

	Cheap range	Popular range	Gift range
Product quantity	100,000	60,000	10,000
Turnover	280,000	258,000	124,000
Total costs	252,000	206,400	74,400
Opportunity cost	25,200	0	0
Profit	53,200	51,600	49,600

The retailer now knows that even if it sells only products from the 'cheap' range, the business profits for the year are protected.

ACTION POINT

Are your product sales subject to customer preference choices? Would you lose significant profits if you were only able to sell the lowest priced products in your range? Would it be worthwhile to add an opportunity cost to the prices of your cheaper products to protect the profitability of your business?

TOP TIPS

When you add an opportunity cost to product prices to protect business profitability, you have to make sure that you are not pricing those products above those of your competitors.

EFFECTS OF CURRENCY EXCHANGE RATES

Looking for extra business can mean addressing overseas opportunities, but you have to then manage the financial impact on your business of dealing with foreign currency because:

- Overseas suppliers will probably expect to be paid in their own currency.
- Overseas customers might want to buy in their own currency.

Foreign currency exchange rates are displayed in business newspapers and television news programmes, but you will probably get more immediate and up-to-date information by looking at the website for your bank.

The daily movement in currency exchange rates can have a significant impact on your prices and profitability. At the time that this book was being written, the following exchange rates, for the British pound, were published:

Currency:	Pound rate:
US Dollar (US$)	1.45
EU Euro (€)	1.13

This means that, at this time:

- £1 would buy 1.45 US dollars (US$).
- £1 would buy 1.13 European euros (€).

For example, if your business imports or exports products to the value of £10,000, the value of the transactions in overseas currencies, at the exchange rates quoted above, can be *calculated as:*

£10,000 x 1.45 = US$14,500
£10,000 x 1.13 = €11,300

Since currency exchange rates change every day, the above calculations can change significantly between the dates of agreeing an order and completing the financial transaction.

🔍 EXAMPLE

Businesses dealing with Zimbabwe during 2008 had to address the falling value of the Zimbabwean dollar that reflected the political crisis in that country. The value of an order with a Zimbabwe business could easily increase by 10% or more in one day because of the loss in the value of Zimbabwe's currency; as a result, few businesses were willing to negotiate with Zimbabwean businesses.

If you can negotiate overseas business in British pounds, you avoid the hassle of dealing with overseas currencies, though it can make your products uncompetitive since overseas businesses are likely to build in an opportunity cost to protect themselves from currency fluctuations.

Many overseas businesses demand that transactions are dealt with in their own currency, which means that if you transact business with an American organisation, payments will be made in US$.

Q CASE STUDY

StoneGlass received an enquiry from a French retail consortium, for products totalling £40,000, with prices quoted in Euros. The Euro price for the order was duly calculated at the current exchange rate of 1.13 as €45,200. Some weeks later, the order was received and the goods were dispatched to France; payment of €45,200 was received against delivery and transferred to the StoneGlass bank which converted at the new current exchange rate of £1 = €1.26 as follows:

$$\frac{45\ 200}{1.26} = £35,873$$

StoneGlass received £35,873 for goods that it had valued at £40,000 and had lost over £4,000 profit on this order.

Currency exchange rates can have a similar effect on goods that you buy from overseas suppliers.

Q CASE STUDY

StoneGlass researched the internet and found an American supplier that could supply glass materials at a delivered price that was 10% cheaper than the present suppliers. They decided to place an initial order for US$58,000 which they calculated, at current exchanges rates, would cost the business £40,000 and would save £4,000 of costs. When the order was delivered StoneGlass asked the bank to transfer US$58,000 to the American supplier, which it did by calculating the amount due at the new current exchange rate of 1.31. The amount debited to the StoneGlass bank account £44,275, which meant that the saving that StoneGlass had expected had been lost.

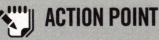

ACTION POINT

Do you or are you likely to deal with overseas businesses? What effect would changing exchange rates have on your business? Carry out a few calculations at various exchange rates higher and lower than the current levels. At what point would an exchange rate make the business unviable?

You can protect your business against exchange rate fluctuations by engaging in advance currency purchase.

Advance currency purchase

When you agree overseas business, you can 'forward buy' currency at a price agreed today. This means that you can quote an order in a currency amount and be confident that any future movements in the exchange rate will not impact on the value you have to pay.

Of course, when you buy forward you can lose the benefit of a movement in the exchange rate that happens to be in your favour!

QUICK RECAP

- *Turnover ratio tells you if your turnover growth is 'real' and reflects an increase in sales and product volumes rather than inflation.*
- *You can protect your business from customers purchasing only low price/low profit items by adding an opportunity cost to your sales prices.*
- *Currency exchange rates can substantially influence the cost of doing business overseas.*
- *You can protect your business from the effects of currency exchange rates by engaging in advance currency purchase.*

CHAPTER 10

Quickstart guide: summary of key points

1. WHAT DOES SUCCESSFUL FINANCE MEAN?

Successful finance means:
- Identifying and acquiring funds for capital resources.
- Providing and managing the cash to finance ongoing operations.
- Keeping effective accounting records.
- Managing cash flow.
- Creating financial competitive advantage.
- Ensuring a balance between income, costs and profit.
- Planning for future operations and growth.

2. IDENTIFYING YOUR COSTS

- Costs can be categorised into the following different groups:
  - Capital costs
  - Revenue costs
  - Direct costs
  - Indirect costs or overheads
  - Fixed costs
  - Variable costs
- Cost categories are not self-exclusive, but different categories are used for different purposes in financial management.
- Costing techniques help you to identify the relationship between income, the cost of producing a product, and the profit contributed to the business.
- Total absorption costing determines the overall total cost of a business unit or product.
- Marginal costing determines the contribution that additional orders make to the organisation.

3. HOW TO CALCULATE AND APPLY BREAK-EVEN POSITIONS

This chapter explained how to calculate:
- Break-even points.
- A break-even point allowing for contingencies.
- Changing values for break-even using a break-even chart.

4. PREPARING ACCURATE AND MEANINGFUL BUDGETS

- A budget is a plan outlining the expected total costs of providing a specific level of products in the next trading period.
- Incremental budgeting involves adding percentage uplifts to a previous year's figures to take account of inflation and additional projected business.
- Zero-based budgeting assumes a nil base for future costs and examines whether expenditure is necessary and, if so, how it can be implemented most cost effectively.
- Contingency budgeting is a way of allowing for unexpected emergencies in the future.
- A budget journal is a tool for recording unexpected events so that potential repeats can be allowed for in subsequent budgets.
- The indiscriminate cutting of well-prepared budgets can create a barrier to business growth and profitability.
- Flexed budgeting provides maximum information to enable decision-makers to achieve optimal results.
- Seasonally analysed budgets provide accurate costs to reflect other seasonal variances.
- Budgetary control aims to check that a business unit has:
  - Achieved the projected level of income.
  - Not exceeded the projected level of expenditure.

- An effective budgetary control system includes a repetitive cycle of actions, including:
  - Setting budget objectives.
  - Measuring actual performance against budget standards.
  - Identifying areas for remedial action.
  - Taking necessary action to correct unexpected trends.
- To support an effective budgetary control system, you first need to implement a number of basic requirements, such as:
  - Involvement of departmental managers in the preparation of budgets.
  - An accurate, reliable and timely system for recording and disseminating actual financial information.
  - Regular monitoring.
  - Willingness to investigate variances.
- The budgetary control cycle is most effectively implemented by the use of variance analysis and particularly of cumulative budget analysis
- In the normal course of business, budget values should *never* be changed.

5. MANAGING THE CASH FLOWING THROUGH YOUR BUSINESS

- You can have a profitable business yet still fail because of poor cash flow.
- In order to manage cash flow, you have to manage your working capital.
- Stocks need to be maintained at an optimum level commensurate with the business unit's level of operation.
- Credit arrangements can destroy your business if they are not managed efficiently.
- Make sure that customers pay accounts on time by assertively chasing overdue accounts.

- A non-paying customer is not an asset to your business – it is a liability that can become a disaster.
- Pay suppliers on time to protect necessary deliveries to your business and to ensure that you have good suppliers in the future.
- A cash flow statement predicts positive or negative cash balances.
- You can choose – create a cash flow statement or organise an overdraft – just remember that the overdraft costs you money and profit!

6. CAPITAL EXPENDITURE AND MANAGING CAPITAL RESOURCES

- You can calculate the value return from capital asset expenditure by calculating the payback value of the investment.
- The internal rate of return on an investment compares average net profit with the cost of the investment.
- A net present value calculation tells you the real return of an investment taking into account inflation.
- To identify the effects of inflation, you can calculate discounted cash flow using an index such as the CPI.
- Capital assets can be managed using a fixed asset register in which you record purchase costs, upgrading costs, annual depreciation and any value received when the asset is eventually sold.

7. UNDERSTANDING FINAL ACCOUNTS

- Information provided in business accounts can be analysed into different sections that are easier to assimilate.

- P&L statements are presented in a traditional format, though businesses might have different sections according to groupings of major costs.
- All businesses invariably show a section that contains direct costs or cost of sales.
- Published accounts often include 'notes' that give more detailed information than the totals shown in the actual statement.
- Balance Sheets are also presented in a traditional format that enables information to be analysed easily.
- Checking the values in account statements between two years can tell you about important movements in the business.
- Comparing the information from a competitor's accounts with that for your own business can indicate issues that you need to address.
- Apply care when looking at data shown in graphical form since it is often more easy to hide questionable performance in eye-catching graphics.
- The information contained in the Annual Report and Accounts for a major corporation provides a great deal of information about the business.

8. KEEPING A CHECK ON TRENDS

- The quality of financial management can be assessed using management ratios to assess whether financial management is becoming more or less efficient.
- Cost and profitability ratios look at how well costs are being managed against the turnover achieved.
- Working capital ratios look at how efficiently the business is managing the cash flowing through it.
- Productivity ratios look at the benefits achieved from the resources employed in the business.
- A ratios table for several trading periods will quickly show the

issues on which you need to concentrate to improve specific areas of your business.

- You do not have to use traditional ratios, but can design your own ratios that more accurately reflect your business operation.
- If you design your own ratios, check that they work by calculating those ratios for past trading periods that you have experienced.

9. MANAGING EXTERNAL FINANCIAL INFLUENCES

- Turnover ratio tells you if your turnover growth is 'real' and reflects an increase in sales and product volumes rather than inflation.
- You can protect your business from customers purchasing only low price/low profit items by adding an opportunity cost to your sales prices.
- Currency exchange rates can substantially influence the cost of doing business overseas.
- You can protect your business from the effects of currency exchange rates by engaging in advance currency purchase.

CHAPTER 11

Troubleshooting

We hope that we have provided enough information, in sufficient detail, to enable you to improve the efficiency of your financial management. However, we have, in the past, received a number of questions about successfully managing finance and we think that it is worthwhile sharing some of them with you.

Q: Surely budgeting is a laborious and time-wasting task; why should I spend so much time trying to guess the future?
A: Budgeting is an opportunity to really understand what makes your business tick and how you can get the best results in the future. If you ignore the budgeting process you reduce your chance of success.

Q: You said that you have to designate capital costs according to the size of the business. How does that work in reality?
A: Businesses often have a benchmark or cut-off rule that is applied to the purchase of long-term equipment. A new business might say that any equipment costing more than £300 will be designated as capital; as the business grows it could increase the benchmark to £500 or even to £1,000.

Q. I notice that you did not include telephone expenses in the list of fixed costs for StoneGlass. I do not understand that because I have a fixed cost contract for my telephone facility.

A: All costs can fall into different categories for different businesses. If you have a fixed cost contract for any service, you will include it in the fixed costs for your business. For example, some businesses contract marketing at a set price for a year, in which case that would become a fixed cost for those businesses.

Q: It is almost impossible for me to get accounting information so it is easier to create a budget using last year's data plus an uplift for inflation, which seems to have worked in the past. Why should I bother to create a more complex budget?

A: It depends on what you and your business want to achieve in terms of future growth and success. If you are sure that you are getting the best possible results, then why change the system? However, if you think that you could achieve more then perhaps you should talk with your boss about getting the information you need.

Q: I find that trying to monitor and control a budget every month is a waste of time because the information I get from the accounts department is always at least one month late and usually incorrect. Is there another way I can implement budgetary control?

A: You cannot control your budget without accurate monthly data about actual expenditure. You need to explain to the person responsible for providing the monthly accounting information what can happen to a business if budget variances are not spotted quickly. Try using the British Airways example given in the book (see page 82).

Q: I know that some of our customers take a long time to pay accounts but we always get the money in the end and I hate chasing people asking for money. What is so bad about allowing a little extra time to pay?

A: Perhaps your business has a fund of spare cash and you do not need to worry about cash flow? If not, you have to think about what is most important to you – your embarrassment or the security of the business? Chasing overdue accounts does not have to be confrontational; you can achieve your aims by maintaining a friendly, yet firm, relationship that includes an agreement to keep the promises made when doing business together – you supply quality products on time and the customer pays on time. Remember that a business can fail through lack of cash flow.

Q: Do I need to calculate management ratios every month?

A: You should use ratios to manage your business unit to the most successful outcomes. Most businesses use budgetary control processes monthly to maintain control over normal operations, then complete ratios at the end of the year to check that overall performance is not deteriorating in some way over the longer term. It depends on you and your business unit – if you find that some aspect of the business somehow evades control every month, the chances are that you need to design and/or use a management ratio to increase control over that aspect of the business, in a similar way to the clothing manufacturer given as an example (see page 188).

Q: Do I have to accept the demands of foreign companies to work in their currencies? Why can't I just use pound sterling values when I deal with overseas countries?

A: You might find some overseas companies willing to accept quotes and invoices in your currency, but you might still find that the final transaction is in the customer or supplier's currency. You can also find that some overseas companies might not deal with you unless you agree to their currencies. In addition, there are certain products that are traded worldwide in a specific currency, usually the US dollar. Ultimately, if you want to do the business you might have to play by the rules.

APPENDICES

APPENDIX A: PROFIT AND LOSS ACCOUNTS FOR STONEGLASS LIMITED

P&L ACCOUNT FOR YEARS 2007 TO 2009 (PLUS BUDGET FOR 2010)

	2007	2008	2009	2010	Revised 2010
Turnover	2,230,000	2,870,000	3,480,000	4,300,000	4,730,000
Direct costs:					
Materials	1,218,000	1,560,000	2,198,000	2,310,000	2,194,500
Wages	367,200	548,500	796,000	850,000	807,500
Employee costs	21,000	31,000	54,800	57,000	54,150
Maintenance	14,700	16,300	23,600	8,000	8,000
Depreciation	10,000	10,000	10,000	73,500	73,500
Electricity	9,600	13,700	18,100	18,000	18,000
Water	1,700	2,800	3,800	2,000	2,000
Consumables	3,600	5,100	8,300	4,000	4,000
Packaging costs	4,500	6,900	8,700	12,000	12,000
Business rates	12,000	16,000	18,600	22,000	22,000
Insurance	9,000	11,600	13,400	15,000	15,000
Total direct costs	1,671,300	2,221,900	3,153,300	3,371,500	3,210,650
Gross profit	558,700	648,100	326,700	928,500	1,519,350
Overheads:					

Owners salaries	120,000	150,000	180,000	200,000	180,000
Admin salaries	32,000	53,000	82,400	90,000	85,500
Employee costs	9,000	14,000	27,400	30,000	28,500
Design costs				80000	80000
Marketing	2,300	6,800	8,100	10,000	10,000
Stationery	600	700	3,400	3,000	3,000
Telephone & post	3,600	5,900	7,600	8,000	8,000
Maintenance	200	600	1,700	2,000	2,000
Employee consumables	700	900	2,300	1,000	1,000
Loan interest	0	0	0	80,000	80,000
Audit	3,500	4,600	6,100	7,000	7,000
Bank charges	2,400	3,300	4,700	5,000	5,000
Total overheads	174,300	239,800	323,700	516,000	490,000
Net profit before tax	384400	408300	3000	412500	1,029,350
Less: Tax	130,000	170,000	4,000	180,000	300,000
Retained profit	254,400	238,300	-1,000	232,500	729,350
Number of employees	12	15	16	24	16

APPENDIX B: BALANCE SHEET FOR YEARS 2007 TO 2009 (PLUS BUDGET FOR 2010)

Fixed assets:	305,000	290,000	275,000	831,500	831,500
Premises	200,000	200,000	200,000	200,000	200,000
Machinery	80,000	70,000	60,000	621,500	621,500
Office	25,000	20,000	15,000	10,000	10,000
Current assets:	539,400	877,700	1,064,300	1,462,700	1,992,050
Inventory	211,600	380,000	492,000	447,000	197,000
Debtors	327,800	497,700	572,300	406,000	400,000
Cash at bank	0	0	0	609,700	1,395,050
Current liabilities:	520,000	605,000	777,600	500,000	300,000
Creditors	353,000	392,000	528,600	500,000	300,000
Bank overdraft	167,000	213,000	249,000	0	0
Long-term liabilities:	0	0	0	1,000,000	1,000,000
Loan	0	0	0	1,000,000	1,000,000
Net assets	324,400	562,700	561,700	794,200	1,523,550
Equity:	324,400	562,700	561,700	794,200	1,523,550
Owners investment	50,000	50,000	50,000	50,000	50,000
Retained profits	274,400	512,700	511,700	744,200	1,473,550

Index

Account statement, 104, 150, 208
Accounting period, 61
Accounting rate of return, 123–124
Accounting records, 5, 6, 11, 40, 81, 93, 120, 136, 204, 206
Accuracy, 19, 24, 25, 28, 33, 36, 37, 38, 41, 51, 57, 58, 65, 71, 72, 73, 76, 80, 81, 87, 90, 93, 99, 146, 147, 191, 205, 206, 209, 213
Actual expenditure, 81, 213
Administration, 5, 7, 13, 17, 19, 26, 30, 35, 38, 39, 43, 59, 61, 62, 63, 96, 136, 139, 140, 143, 170, 180, 182
Apportioning costs, 19, 25–29, 33, 34, 37, 45
  Employee working hours, 28
  Machine capacity, 26–27
  Space, 25–26

Balance sheet, 97, 135, 136, 137, 140, 141–145, 149, 208, 218
  Added value, 97, 143
  Current assets, 142, 143, 144, 185, 218
  Current liabilities, 97, 142, 143, 144, 185, 218
  Fixed assets, 142, 143, 144, 185, 218
  Long term liabilities, 142, 143, 144, 185, 218
  Owners' equity, 143
Bank manager, 2, 144
Break-even chart, 52–54, 55, 205
Break-even point, 22, 47, 48, 49, 50, 51, 52, 54, 55, 205
Budget, 21, 38, 57–94, 95, 112, 114, 116, 152, 153, 174, 181, 183, 184, 185, 187, 188, 205–206, 212, 213
Budget journal, 69, 70–71, 93, 205
Budget manager, 81, 60, 64, 68, 71, 72, 73, 74, 90, 92, 93, 206
Budget monitoring, 81, 90, 94, 206, 213
Budget statement, 59, 61, 72, 113
Budgetary control, 57, 68, 76, 80–83, 84, 87, 89, 90, 91, 93, 94, 95, 205, 206, 213, 214
  Budgetary control cycle, 80, 93, 94, 206
  Performance, 73, 74, 80, 84, 93, 206

  Standards and objectives, 8, 58, 80, 93, 206
  Budgetary control process, 78, 87, 91, 214
Business performance, 60, 64, 73, 74, 80, 83, 84, 93, 140, 141, 145, 146, 147, 151, 152, 174, 189, 190, 206
Business structure, 81

Capital, 7, 11, 23, 76, 155, 157, 158, 187, 204
Capital assets, 6, 17, 29, 30, 74, 97, 111, 112, 119, 120, 122, 124, 125, 129–130, 132, 134, 159, 163, 167, 170, 207
  Disposing of, 132, 133
  Purchasing, 6, 15, 16, 111, 112, 120, 129
  Value, 29, 30, 31, 32, 120, 121, 134, 207
Capital costs, 15–16, 17, 24, 29, 46, 204, 212
Capital expenditure (CAPEX), 16, 17, 60, 76, 112, 119–134, 207
  Capital expenditure budget, 60
Capital gearing ratio, 156, 157, 158
Cash, 5, 7, 11, 89, 95, 96, 101, 102, 110, 112, 116, 119, 121, 143, 144, 159, 160, 161, 163, 164, 204, 208, 213
Cash investment, 6
Cash flow, 7, 8, 9, 38, 95–117
  Effect of credit arrangements, 104, 103
  Inflow and outflow, 111, 114
Cash flow forecast, 78, 112–116
Cash flow management, 6, 7, 11, 95, 111–117, 204, 206, 208
Changing budget analysis, 90–92, 94, 206
Competition, 10, 19, 33, 37, 45, 63, 68, 71, 73, 121, 140, 141, 143, 144, 145, 150, 152, 196, 198, 199, 208
Competitive costing, 33–34
Contingency allowance, 51, 52, 55, 71, 72, 73, 205
Contingency budgeting, 68–69, 93, 205
Cost effective, 64, 65, 68, 71, 93, 129, 205
Costs, 7, 8–10, 11, 13–46, 47, 52, 53, 54, 58, 59, 60, 61, 63, 64, 65, 69, 73, 76, 77, 78, 80, 81, 82, 87, 93, 102, 103, 117, 120, 123, 130, 132, 134, 136, 140, 141,

149, 152, 166, 174, 178, 191, 196, 201, 204, 205, 207, 208, 212
Capital costs and revenue costs, 15–16, 17, 20, 24, 29, 46, 204, 212
Direct costs and indirect costs, 15, 17–19, 20, 23, 24, 25, 30, 33, 34, 35, 36, 37, 38, 40, 41, 61, 136, 140, 141, 149, 164, 166, 174, 175, 204, 208
Fixed costs and variable costs, 15, 20, 21–23, 25, 41, 42, 43, 44, 46, 47, 48, 49, 50, 51, 53, 54, 112, 204, 212
Revenue costs, 15, 16, 17, 18, 21, 38
Cost centres, 14–15, 17, 18, 21, 38
Costing systems, 38–45, 46, 68, 204
Contribution, 43–45
Marginal costing, 42–43
Total absorption costing, 38–42, 47
Creditors, 97, 102, 107, 108, 109, 110–111, 142, 144, 162, 163, 164, 165, 166, 169, 171, 173, 176, 177, 183, 185, 186, 218
Aged creditors analysis, 111
Creditors diary, 111
Reputation, 111
Suppliers, 111
Creditor management ratio, 162–163
Credit, 102–104, 106, 111, 113, 116, 117, 161, 162, 163, 176, 177, 182, 206
Cumulative budget analysis, 87, 88–89, 94, 206
Currency exchange rate effects, 194, 198–201, 209, 214
Advance currency purchase, 201
Current assets, 97, 158, 159
Current liabilities, 97, 158, 159, 160
Customer purchasing preferences, 194, 196–198

Debtors, 97, 102–110, 116, 142, 144, 161, 162, 163, 164, 165, 166, 169, 171, 173, 176, 177, 182, 183, 185, 186, 218
Aged debtor analysis, 106
Credit, 103–104
Customers, 103–107
Debtor accounts, 104–108, 162, 183
Debtors' diary, 104–105, 106
Debt collection agency, 108
Debtor management ratio, 161–162
Departmental costs, 14, 17, 18, 21, 22, 38, 41, 47, 48
Depreciation, 29–33, 130, 132, 133–134,

143, 178, 207
Cumulative, 30–31
Straight line, 31–33
Designing ratios, 188–190, 191, 209, 214
Discounted cash flow, 125, 126–127, 134, 207
Discounted prices, 44, 84, 86, 89, 92, 182

Equipment, 5, 7, 15, 23, 24, 29, 30, 59, 120, 121, 122, 128, 129, 167, 183, 212
Expenses, 7, 9, 16, 21, 212
External financial influences, 193–201, 209
Economic, 193
Political, 193
Socio-economic, 193
Technological, 193
PEST/ STEP factors, 194

Final accounts, 135–150, 207–208
Financial competitive advantage, 5, 11, 204
Financial operating resources, 6–7
Fixed assets, 120, 121, 139, 140, 142, 143, 144, 146, 157, 167, 170, 171, 173, 178, 185, 179, 186, 204, 218
Internal rate of return, 121, 125, 127, 134, 207
Net present value, 121, 125, 127, 134, 207
Purchasing, 121
Payback value, 121–123, 124, 134, 207
Register, 130, 131, 132, 133, 134, 207
Flexed budgeting, 61, 73–76, 80, 93, 122, 182, 205
Achievable budget, 73, 74
Optimistic budget, 74
Pessimistic budget, 74
Forward plan, 5, 6, 8
Funds, 6, 11, 33, 58, 63, 121, 155, 187, 188, 190, 204, 213

Gearing ratio, 173, 186, 187, 188, 190
Addressing, 187–188
Generating profits vs generating cash flow, 95, 96
Graphics, 147, 150, 208
Growth, 6, 11, 73, 74, 93, 138, 144, 157, 194, 195, 196, 201, 204, 205, 209, 212, 213

Hidden allowance, 68

HM Customs and Excise, 139
HM Revenue and Customs, 16, 29, 30

Incremental budgeting, 61–63, 66, 67, 68, 80, 93, 205
Inflation, 61, 63, 65, 66, 67, 68, 93, 125, 126, 127, 128, 129, 134, 195, 196, 201, 205, 207, 209, 212
Inflation index, 125, 126, 127, 128, 134, 195, 207
   Consumer Price Index (CPI), 125, 126, 129, 134, 207
   Retail Price Index (RPI), 125
Insurance, 19, 21, 24, 26, 28, 63, 78
Interest, 3, 21, 76, 77, 78, 102, 103, 110, 111, 116, 120, 122, 136, 155, 156, 166, 188
Inventory, 97, 98–102, 144, 159, 160, 163, 164, 165, 166, 176, 183
   Annual stock check, 99
   Managing, 98–100, 102, 103
Invoice, 34, 104, 105, 106, 107, 108, 109, 110, 132, 136, 214
Invoice discounting, 108–109
Invoice factoring, 108–109

Large corporate accounts, 145–149
   Account highlights, 145, 146
   Executive reports, 145, 147–148
   Notes to accounts, 148
Loan, 3, 6, 16, 21, 60, 76, 77, 78, 97, 111, 116, 120, 122, 124, 136, 141, 143, 144, 155, 156, 157, 177, 187, 188
Long term liabilities, 45, 82
Loss leaders, 45, 82

Maintenance, 7, 26, 27, 30, 59, 76, 77, 78, 112, 129, 130, 132
Manager, 1, 14, 33, 37, 60, 64, 68, 71, 72, 73, 74, 81, 83, 86, 89, 90, 92, 93, 110, 121, 152, 170, 193, 206
Management accounts, 83, 136, 137, 183
Management performance, 172–180
Management ratios, 151, 152–158, 166, 189, 191, 194, 208, 214
   Return on capital employed (ROCE), 154, 155
Marketing, 5, 7, 9, 13, 21, 69, 74, 86, 140, 141, 212
Net present value (NPV), 121, 125, 127,

134, 207
Non-Executive Directors (NEDs), 148

Operational costs, 5, 11, 19, 24, 25, 47, 61, 80, 140
Operating resources, 6–7, 9
Opportunity costs, 123, 189, 196, 197, 198, 199, 201, 209
Outsourcing, 38
Overdraft, 97, 102, 104, 111, 114, 116, 117, 143, 144, 166, 177, 207
Overdue accounts, 106, 107, 108, 117, 162, 206, 213
Overheads, 7, 18, 19, 20, 30, 33, 34, 35, 36, 37, 38, 40, 45, 46, 136, 141, 153, 174, 175, 178, 204
Over inflated budget, 71
Owners' equity, 156, 157

Payback value, 121–123, 124, 134, 207
   Opportunity costs, 123, 189, 196, 197, 198, 199, 201, 209
Percentage uplifts/additions, 33, 61, 63, 65, 93, 205
Planning improvements, 180–187
Premises costs, 25–26
Price levels, 37, 36, 38, 40, 41, 43, 44, 45, 49, 51, 52, 63, 64, 65, 67–68, 71, 82, 85, 86, 87, 89, 130, 178, 180, 181, 182, 189, 194, 195, 196, 197, 198, 200, 201, 209, 212
Products, 7, 9, 13, 14, 17, 18, 19, 20, 22, 26, 27, 28, 30, 33, 34, 36, 37, 38, 40, 44, 45, 46, 48, 49, 65, 67, 93, 95, 96, 97, 98, 100, 104, 111, 112, 120, 139, 140, 143, 147, 152, 164, 166, 167, 170, 178, 180, 182, 187, 188, 189
Productivity ratios, 152, 166, 167–172, 173, 179, 186, 191, 208
   Employee productivity ratio, 168
   Fixed asset productivity ratio, 167–168, 169, 171
   Payroll productivity ratio, 170–171
   Performance, 178
Profit, 2, 6, 7, 8–10, 11, 20, 32, 36, 37, 39, 40, 41, 44, 45, 46, 47, 49, 50, 51, 58, 60, 68, 76, 82, 89, 95, 96, 104, 112, 117, 122, 123, 124, 125, 126, 127, 128, 132, 134, 140, 141, 143, 144, 152, 153, 154, 155, 156, 158, 163, 167, 168, 169,

170, 171, 172, 174, 175, 176, 178, 179,
181, 187, 189, 196, 197, 200, 201, 204,
207, 209
Profit contingency, 51–52
Profit margin, 41, 50, 125, 196
Profit retention, 140, 144
Profit & loss account, 35, 135, 136, 137–
141, 143, 149, 184, 208, 216
  Cost of sales, 20, 41, 136, 138, 140,
  149, 153, 208
  Cost of administration, 136, 140, 143
  Total income, 39, 54, 140, 146
  Value of profit retained, 140
Profitability, 8, 47, 57, 61, 73, 82, 83, 93,
141, 147, 152, 167, 174, 175, 180, 188,
196, 197, 198, 205, 208

Resources, 2, 5, 6, 8, 9, 11, 15, 57, 58, 59,
69, 73, 74, 119, 121, 167, 170, 172, 178,
191, 204, 207, 208
Revenue, 9, 15, 16, 17, 20, 23, 46, 59, 70,
204
Risk, 10, 19, 24, 74, 103, 107, 110, 111,
116, 157

Safe budget, 71, 72, 73
Salaries, 18, 20, 21, 23, 25, 28, 33, 38, 59,
63, 67, 73, 78, 139, 148, 170, 171, 172,
178, 181, 183
Seasonally analysed budgeting, 76–79,
93, 105
  Seasonalisation, 76, 80, 112,
  Working days, 77, 78, 101
Selling price, 36, 38, 40, 41, 45
Shortfalls, 7, 112, 116
Size of business, 16, 21, 33, 38, 57, 60, 68,
100, 102, 109, 121, 129, 145, 146, 166,
170, 172, 212
Small business, 33, 129, 161, 167
Stock, 86, 98–102, 117, 120, 144, 159,
163, 166, 176, 181, 183, 188, 206
  Control, 98, 99, 102, 163
  Excessive, 102, 187
  Levels, 98, 100, 101
  Operational needs, 99, 100–102, 117

Records, 98–99, 100, 101
Suppliers, 7, 65, 85, 86, 97, 98, 99, 100,
101, 102, 103, 110, 111, 112, 113, 114,
116, 117, 130, 133, 160, 163, 164, 166,
176, 177, 181, 182, 183, 198, 200, 207,
214
  Quality, 64, 65

Trading period, 10, 29, 49, 50, 51, 58, 91,
93, 99, 128, 132, 136, 137, 138, 140,
141, 143, 144, 172, 190, 191, 194, 205,
208, 209
Trial balance, 136
Turnover, 9, 50, 68, 69, 76, 86, 139, 140,
161, 162, 167, 168, 169, 170, 171, 174,
175, 176, 177, 182, 191, 194, 197, 208
Turnover ratio, 194–196, 201, 209

Value return, 134, 207
Variance analysis, 83–87, 94, 194, 206,
213
  Revised budget policy, 86, 188
  Variances from budget, 90, 91

Wages (see also salaries), 7, 21, 23, 25, 28,
38, 39, 40, 42, 59, 62, 66, 67, 70, 75, 84,
113, 114, 138, 139, 170, 171, 172, 178,
183, 184, 216
Working capital, 7, 95, 96–98, 117, 124,
158–167, 187, 206
  Management, 96–98
Working capital ratios, 152, 158–167,
177, 191, 208
  Acid test or quick ratio, 159–161, 162,
  163, 165, 169, 171, 173, 176, 177, 186
  Current ratio, 158–159, 160, 161, 162,
  163, 165, 169, 171, 173, 177, 186
  Inventory management ratio, 163–166

Zero-based budgeting, 61, 64–68, 74, 80,
93, 180, 181, 182, 205
  Zero/Nil base, 64
  Budget database, 64